Building the House Church is a manual for how to begin or develop a house church or other small group within the larger church. The book shows systematically how a group of Christians small enough to fit into a living room can be the church.

A key concept of the book is covenant, deciding intentionally who we want to be in relationship to Christ and to each other. Sample covenants and stories of house churches involved in covenant writing provide help to groups interested in creating their own covenant.

Included in the book are practical ideas on worshiping with a small group, meeting the needs of children, managing conflict, reaching consensus, and pastoral care—ideas growing out of the author's experiences in house churches and small groups.

Like the house churches of the New Testament, modern house churches are finding that the essential functions of the church can happen in the small group—and happen well.

"I believe," writes Lois Barrett, "that in the house church, the face-to-face church, Christians can be the church. In fact, the house church provides a context which can make it easier for us to be the church: to worship, to teach and learn, to disciple each other, to share with each other, to be in mission together, and to make decisions together."

D0066777

BUILDING THE HOUSE CHURCH

Lois Barrett

HERALD PRESS
Scottdale, Pennsylvania
Kitchener, Ontario
1986

Library of Congress Cataloging-in-Publication Data

Barrett, Lois.
    Building the house church.

    Bibliography: p.
    1. House churches.   I. Title.
BV601.85.B38   1986   253.7´6   86-14324
ISBN 0-8361-3415-X (pbk.)

BUILDING THE HOUSE CHURCH
Copyright © 1986 by Herald Press, Scottdale, Pa. 15683
    Published simultaneously in Canada by Herald Press,
    Kitchener, Ont. N2G 4M5. All rights reserved.
Library of Congress Catalog Card Number: 86-14324
International Standard Book Number: 0-8361-3415-X
Printed in the United States of America
Design by Gwen Stamm

86 87 88 89 90 9 8 7 6 5 4 3 2 1

To the people of
Mennonite Church of the Servant,
who have worked with me
in building house churches

Contents

"And in him [Christ]
you too are being built together
to become a dwelling
in which God lives by his Spirit"

(Eph. 2:22, NIV).

Preface

I have often had to explain what a house church is. I discovered while I was in seminary that many of my classmates had never heard of house churches. What had been so important in my experience in a house church was a new idea to them. Some of these students were preparing to leave to start churches but had never heard of the option of starting house churches—or had no idea how to begin. In addition to seminary students, many other people have the notion that "church" is what happens on Sunday morning with 200 people. Smaller groupings that meet at other times may be beneficial, but are not really church, these people would say.

This book grows out of the need to present a model of being the church which emphasizes covenant, commitment, and personal involvement with a small number of people. I have tried to offer the house church not just as an acceptable model of the church, but indeed as a good way of being the church, where Christians can emphasize the essentials of being the church—covenanting, worshiping, teaching, sharing, discipling, deciding, using spiritual gifts, serving, and growing. I have found that these essentials can be present in the church whether the church has seven or seventy people, and whether or not the church has a regular meeting place or an organ or ten Sunday school classes. Like the New Testament house churches, modern house churches have discovered that we—the people—are the stones which build up the church of Christ.

The house church is not just an alternative church for the avant-garde. It is a way of being church that seeks to live out the New Testament vision of the church. Whether the total congregation is small (a single house church) or large (made up of many house churches), the house church model can help congregations experience church in new ways.

Larger congregations may wish to reevaluate what is happening within the small groups of various kinds already present within the church and see if their functions can be expanded (or recognized to exist already) to include more of what it means to be the church. Or larger congregations may wish to subdivide into a number of house churches. "Fellowships" that are meeting regularly but have not chosen to call themselves "church" may wish to look again at what the essential functions of the church are to see if they cannot be the church without the negative connotations that certain "sanctuary" traditions hold for them.

Much of what I have written grows out of the experience of Mennonite Church of the Servant in Wichita, an assembly of five houses, of which I am mentor, or teaching minister. I am also grateful for the help of people in many other house churches around North America who responded to my questionnaire and wrote about their experiences, some of which have been included in this book.

Special thanks should go to David Habegger, out of whose vision Mennonite Church of the Servant grew nine years ago and who encouraged me in writing this book. My thanks also goes to Leland Harder, in whose seminary class I wrote the prospectus for this book.

My hope is that this book will be good news to those who are thinking about starting house churches and to those who have already begun and want guidance on how to keep on building the dwelling place of God's Spirit.

—Lois Barrett
Wichita, Kansas

BUILDING THE HOUSE CHURCH

Chapter 1

House Churches

The nine people sitting in a circle in Sharon and Jim's living room sang, "There's a Church Within Us, O Lord." Then Marie said, "It's time for prayer concerns."

"I'm still waiting for word from the public schools on whether I've been hired," said Jan. "It's getting closer and closer to the beginning of school, and I'm worried. I'd like your prayers that I can keep from getting too tied up in knots as I go about this job search."

"Lord, hear our prayer," the rest of the people responded.

"Let us pray for the people of El Salvador," said Dick. "The war has really come home to me this week, since I heard that a friend with whom I went to college was killed by the government forces there."

"Shall we pray for you, too?" interjected Ralph. "For your loss of your friend?"

"Yes, that would be good," said Dick.

"Lord, hear our prayer," they said.

These nine people have covenanted with God and each other to be the church. Their style of church is the house church. They are not primarily an encounter group, although the face-to-face quality of their relationships is emotionally supportive and therapeutic.

They are not primarily a fellowship group, although they have a lot of potluck meals together and volleyball games and weekend retreats.

They are not primarily a strategy for starting new large churches, although house churches may be new church-planting efforts.

They are not primarily a Bible study group, although they do spend a significant amount of time in Bible study and doing theology.

They are not primarily a mission task force, although they may have a common local mission as a house church.

They are not primarily a first level of decision-making for the larger cluster of house churches of which they are a part, although they do process issues that will come before the larger church for decision.

They are, above all, a church. As a church they worship, eat the Lord's Supper, study, share, pray, listen, confront, encourage, engage in mission, decide, and play with each other.

A house church is a group of people small enough to meet face-to-face, who have covenanted with God and each other to be the church under the authority of Christ and the guidance of the Spirit. A house church often meets in homes, although it may sometimes meet in public buildings. But more important than the place of meeting is the closeness of relationships implied by the word "house."

Can a living-room-size group of people be the church? When Mennonite Church of the Servant in Wichita, Kansas, started under denominational sponsorship as a house church in 1976, we fielded many questions about who we were. Informed by traditional church-planting strategy that saw the first step as buying or constructing or at least renting a meeting house, many people asked us, "When are you going to become a 'real' church?"

"We are a real church," we explained. "You can be the church wherever you meet. The church is a people, not a place."

I have sometimes explained the difference between the house church and a sanctuary church as a difference in place. The place does create an atmosphere which encourages certain kinds of relating to each other and discourages other kinds of relating. Place creates certain kinds of expectations as to what will happen there. But now, I'm moving more toward seeing the "house" as a symbol for the issue of size, which is the real issue.

Size makes a difference in what happens. I know through my own experience and through reading the studies of social scientists that smaller groups allow people to participate more in what is going on. The smaller the church, the closer the interaction. In small groups, people develop closer relationships. They are more accountable to each other. It is more difficult to ignore each other or to act in impersonal ways. If one person is absent, he or she is missed.

A number of studies have shown that, the smaller the group, the more opportunity the individual has for talking or participating in group activities. One study of Baptist churches showed that the smaller the church, the more money given per person.

So when we talk about the house church, we imply much more than a place of meeting. We imply a size of group—small enough to meet in a house, usually from seven to twelve people. We imply a quality of relationship—caring for the whole person as if we lived in the same household. (Some house churches may live in the same household; others have separate households.) We imply a level of participation. In a household, everyone who lives there participates in cooking meals and doing chores as they are able. There are no observers in a household. Even someone who is sick is a vital part of the household and influences the workings of the household. In the house church, members are not Sunday morning observers, but both givers and receivers in worship, teaching, discipling, discerning, and service.

The house church is not the only size group in which church happens, but it is the basic group. The house church is church.

The History of the House Church

Modern house churches have many models in history. The most well known have been the house churches of the New Testament. The earliest Christian churches met in homes. Acts 2:41-47 tells of the believers in Jerusalem who were together and broke bread in their homes daily. In Acts 12:12, the believers gathered for prayer at the house of Mary, the mother of John Mark. In Philippi (Acts 16:15, 40), Thessalonica (Acts 17:7ff.), Corinth (1 Cor. 16:15), Ephesus, Troas, Rome, and wherever the Christian movement spread, small house churches came into existence. Paul's letters refer to these groups as the "church that meets in their [Priscilla and Aquila's] house" (Rom. 16:5; 1 Cor. 16:19) or "Nympha and the church in her house" (Col. 4:15) or "the church that meets in your home" (Philem. 2).

In these churches in the house, people ate meals together in continuation of the tradition of the Lord's Supper. They sang. They taught each other by giving opportunity for each to offer "a hymn, a lesson, a revelation, a tongue, or an interpretation" (1 Cor. 14:26). They prayed. They made decisions. They admonished those who were going astray (1 Cor. 5). They referred to each other as brothers and sisters (1 Cor. 8:12; Eph. 6:23; Phil. 4:1; Col. 1:2; 1 Thess. 5:26-27). The church in the house took on the characteristics of a common household, not only with familial terms for each other, but with familial love for each other (Rom. 12:10). They argued with each other.

Robert Banks has suggested in the book *Paul's Idea of Community*[1] that the quarreling among those who belonged to Paul or to Apollos or to Peter (1 Cor. 1:10ff.) referred to various house churches in Corinth that owed their existence to the work of different apostles. Banks has also suggested that the references to the "whole church" in Corinth (1 Cor. 14:23; Rom. 16:23) mean that these house churches occasionally came together for a joint assembly in the home of Gaius, probably a person of status who could provide enough space for such a meeting.

These churches continued meeting in houses through at least the second century. In the *Martyrdom of Justin*, chapter 2, Justin told the prefect that the Christians do not "all meet in the very same place." He said, "I live above one Martinus, at the Timiotinian Bath; and during the whole time (and I am now living in Rome for the second time), I am unaware of any other meeting than his." The *Clementine Recognitions* (10:71) refer to the generosity of Theophilus of Antioch, who "with all eagerness of desire consecrated the great palace of his house under the name of a church."[2]

Archaeological excavations show houses that were used for worship and later remodeled for larger assemblies of the church, or sanctuary-type buildings built over them on the same site, as the church of Saint Clement in Rome. Excavations in Dura-Europos (on the Euphrates River, now in Syria) have uncovered a private house in which one room had been converted to a small Christian meeting place. At some later time, about A.D. 240, a partition was removed between two other rooms to make a room five meters wide and fifteen meters long for the Christian assembly. The house evidently belonged to a well-to-do citizen of Dura who first offered one room for the meetings of the church and later turned over a large part of the house to the church.

By the latter part of the third century, Christians began building sanctuaries for worship, patterned after the Roman basilica. The basilica was a rectangular building with nave and side aisle, used for a variety of purposes. Its shape has been characteristic of the sanctuary church ever since its adaptation to Christian use at that time. Just as the house as location for the Christian assemblies influenced what happened there, so the basilica, or sanctuary, was a symbol of a different way for the church to function.

John W. Miller has pointed out[3] that, whereas the early house churches governed themselves on the basis of a group process outlined in Matthew 18, already in the second century there was a shift from this congregational style of government to rule by a solitary bishop who was thought of as standing in the place of Jesus himself. "Hence you should know," wrote Cyprian, third-century bishop of Carthage, "that the bishop is in the church and the church is in the bishop, and that if anyone be not with the bishop he is not in the church."

As the center of worship moved from the house fellowship to the altar, the Lord's Supper became not a fellowship meal, but a rite of the altar. Bread and wine were increasingly viewed as holy substances, dispensed by the priests as the "medicine of immortality," as Irenaeus phrased it.

"To share 'in Christ,' " Miller has written, "no longer meant to unite in fellowship with a small group of Christ's people. Now all that was necessary was to come to the bishop, listen to his voice, and receive the sacraments. As ever larger numbers of people joined the church after its alliance with the Roman state, this could be done far more conveniently in large sanctuaries than in houses. With this shift in understanding as to what it meant to be a Christian, the house church had become obsolete.

Throughout the centuries, renewal movements within Christianity have rediscovered the house church in the pages of the New Testament. Monastic movements often worshiped in small groups and emphasized discipline and accountability. Martin Luther, in the early years of his reformation of the church, longed to revive the house church as a major pattern of congregational life. In his preface to "The German Mass and Order of Service (1526), he suggested that those who "want to be Christians in earnest and profess the gospel with hand and mouth should sign their names and meet alone in a house somewhere to pray, to read, to baptize, to receive the sacrament, and to do other Christians works." Moreover, "those who do not lead Christian lives could be known, reproved, corrected, cast out, or excommunicated, according to the rule of Christ (Matt. 18). Here would be no need of much and elaborate singing. Here one could set up an ... order for baptism and the sacrament and center everything on the Word, prayer, and love." Luther, however, never thought it possible to realize his dream for the house church. "I have not yet the people or persons for it, nor do I see many who want it," he lamented.

What Luther despaired of bringing to reality (and later set aside entirely) the Radical Reformers of the sixteenth century put into practice as they met in homes, caves, and other places of protection from persecution. The house as a location for worship and teaching was more than a hiding place from heresy-hunting authorities. The house was again a symbol for the committed believers who cared for each other, admonished each other, and both gave and received in their meetings for worship.

Ambrosius Spitelmaier, interrogated in 1527 on where the Anabaptists came together and what they did, answered,

> They have no special gathering places. When there is peace and unity and when none of those who have been baptized are scat-

tered, they come together wherever the people are. They send messages to each other by a boy or girl. When they have come together they teach one other the divine Word and one asks the other: how do you understand this saying? Thus there is among them a diligent living according to the divine word.[4]

Leopold Scharnschlager, another Anabaptist, taught in 1540:

> Because of the various kinds of temptations spreading everywhere, it is necessary that the called, pledged, and committed members of Jesus Christ should not, as far as they are able, abandon the meetings, wherever they are in the world and in distress (Heb. 10:25). Rather, wherever and however they can—depending on the place and the extent of persecution—they should gather for the sake of love of Christ, be they few or many—2, 3, 4, 6, 10, 15, or 20—more or less. This should be done with wisdom, humility, reason, discipline, amity, and discretion, the more so as we realize that the day of the Lord is near. The Lord says: "Where two or three are gathered in my name, there am I in the midst of them" (Matt. 18:10).[5]

In the seventeenth century, Quakers in England and Pietists on the continent returned to the practice of house meetings.

Methodists also found their origin in the house meeting. The classes appointed by John Wesley were, in effect, little churches. Beginning in 1742, the class meetings became a means of spiritual oversight for Methodist recruits. In the meetings, twelve members met each week with their leader, who questioned them about their spiritual progress. Gradually, the class became less a court of inquiry and more a family circle. Wesley wrote:

> Many now happily experienced that Christian fellowship of which they had not so much an idea as before. They began to

"bear one another burthens," and naturally to "care for each other." As they had a more intimate acquaintance with, so they had a more endeared affection for, each other. And "speaking the truth in love, they grew up into Him in all things who is the Head, even Christ; from whom the whole body, fitly joined together, and compacted by that which every joint supplied, according to the effectual working in measure of every part, increased unto the edifying of itself in love."[6]

These classes and the smaller "bands" into which the classes were divided, functioned as house churches, for the sake of pastoral care, for collection of money, for mutual confession, and for worship. They were the strength of the Methodist movement.

The House Church Today

Renewal is coming to Christianity through house churches in the twentieth century. Modern interest in the house church arose from the experiments of an Anglican parish priest, Ernest Southcott, described in his book *The Parish Comes Alive*.[7] From there the Department of Laity of the World Council of Churches picked up the idea, and the chairman of that department, Hans-Ruedi Weber, published an article on house churches.[8]

Today house churches are meeting among Lutherans and Methodists, Disciples, and Mennonites. Roman Catholic basic ecclesial communities study the Word together in Brazil and Los Angeles. Christians meet in homes in the People's Republic of China. House churches find a home in Japan, the Philippines, and Spain.

Around the world, house churches are functioning as means of church renewal. Where people search for Christian community in the context of an impersonal world, they find "family" in the house church. They are finding that they can be the church wherever "two or three are gathered" in Jesus' name.

I believe that, in the house church, the face-to-face church, Christians can be the church. In fact, the house church provides a context which can make it easier for us to be the church: to worship, to teach and learn, to discipline each other, to share with each other, to be in mission together, and to make decisions together. The rest of this book will look at how the house church can help us in each of these tasks of the church.

Reflection and Action

The following questions (and those at the end of each chapter) may be used for group discussion if you are studying this book with your house church or other small group. Or if you are reading this book alone, you may wish to use these questions as a basis for journaling.

1. Make a list of the activities of the church in which you currently participate or which are important to you: Sunday school classes, women's or men's groups, committees, fellowship groups, sharing groups, house churches, and so on. Now write beside them the function of these activities *for you*. In what way are these groups church for you? For example:

Music committee   Provides a small group of people who meet regularly, whom I can get to know well while we engage in a common task *(not, picks out special music)*

2. Study the New Testament references to the house church found in Romans 16; Acts 2:41-47; Acts 12:12; Acts 15:5ff.; Acts 16:15 and 40; Colossians 4:15; and Philemon 2. How do you think being a house church helped the church deal with

new believers? with Christians who were involved in immorality (1 Cor. 5)? with helping many people feel a part of the worship service (1 Cor. 14:26-33)? with persecution? with poverty among Christians?

3. What do you think is necessary in order to be the church? What is most important to you? What of these things have you done in a large group? What of these things have you done in a small group?

Chapter 2

Covenant

"Is 'house church' really the best name for groups like yours?" a friend once asked me. "Not all these churches actually meet in houses."

I agreed that they did not.

"So what is the common denominator?" he wondered.

We decided that one thing all house churches have in common is a covenant.

The house church is an intentional church. People are not members of the church by accident or without thought or commitment. House churches do not come into being by simply adopting denominational statements of faith and committee structures. House churches are intentional about who they are and what is the basis for their being together. The who, what, why, and sometimes even the how are stated in a covenant.

Any group with a sense of "groupness" has a set of guidelines, written or unwritten. These guidelines define who is in the group and on what basis people enter or leave the group. The guidelines also say how members of the group are to relate to each other; that is, they talk about expected behavior. They usually say something about the reason for the group's existence, its mission in the world. These guidelines set boundaries for the group.

Boundaries may seem limiting, but they are really freeing. Without these boundaries or guidelines, we would spend a lot of time wondering about what was expected and just wandering without a sense of direction.

Sometimes churches try to operate without clear guidelines or without a covenant. One new house church began with high expectations and denominational support for leadership. The initial group of people that gathered was diverse: some Protestant, some Catholic, one Buddhist. Not wanting to offend anyone, the group never did come to agreement on a covenant. There were no boundaries. Because there was no basis for excluding anyone, there was also no basis for including anyone. The group dissolved after a few years without ever becoming a church.

It is good for the church to be inclusive on issues of race, gender, age, and so forth. But on the basic issue of faith and the purpose of the church, churches need a clear center—a goal toward which every member of the church commits himself or herself to be moving. That goal, that center, can be expressed in a written covenant.

Covenant in the Bible

Covenant is an idea basic to the biblical faith. The Old Testament expresses humanity's relationship to God in terms of covenants: with Noah, with Abraham, with Moses and the people of Israel, with David's dynasty. In the ancient near East, a covenant was like a treaty. It established the terms of relationship between two parties. It said how the two intended to relate to each other. Often it ended with a list of the benefits if one lived according to the covenant and the penalties for breaking the covenant. The Mosaic law had a long list of ethical obligations of the covenant. It spelled out the terms of the covenant in great detail. But the essence of the covenant was the relationship it established; it specified with whom one would be in relationship. In Joshua 24, the primary question was, Which god will you choose to serve? The tribes of Israel answered, "We . . . will serve the Lord [Yahweh], for he is our God" (v. 18).

In the New Testament, Jesus inaugurates a new covenant, "the new covenant in my blood" (1 Cor. 11:25). In that new covenant Jesus calls us to establish the relationship of love with neighbor and with God—to be friends of God (John 15:15; James 2:23).

Both Testaments associate covenant with law—ethics and standards of behavior. But even more basic to covenant is the idea that to establish a covenant is to establish a relationship. To live according to the covenant is more than just following certain rules; it is to live in such a way that the relationship continues and grows.

Structures for Relationship

That kind of relationship is what house church covenants are about. A covenant says, first of all, with whom we are in relationship, and second, something about what we need to do to live in those relationships. Covenants need not be long or complicated. They do need to define relationships.

With whom are we in relationship? Covenants deal with the ultimate question: our relationship to God, the God we know in a unique way through Jesus of Nazareth. A church covenant should be clear about where our ultimate allegiance lies. In such a sense, a covenant *is* exclusive. The God of the Bible demands exclusive loyalty. By declaring our allegiance to that God, we exclude allegiance to other gods.

Covenants also say something about our relationships to the church, those other people who have also covenanted with the one God, those people whom we call brothers and sisters in the divine family. Our covenant with God as Parent puts us in familial relationship with other people whom God has chosen and who have chosen God.

Covenants also speak of our relationship to the world, the whole of humanity whom God loves, even though they may not have accepted God's offer of covenant relationship.

The second question church covenants usually answer is, What do we need to do to live out these relationships? If covenants are to make a difference in how we act, it is helpful if they spell out the specifics of relationship. Sometimes these actions are painted in broad strokes in the covenant itself. Our covenant at Mennonite Church of the Servant commits us to "sharing our decisions, our talents, our time, and our possessions." But the nitty-gritty of specific actions is often put into a separate section, or document, called the "understandings." The understandings tell what we mean by the broad and ultimate statements of the covenant.

For example, our covenant commits us to "sharing our decisions." The understandings spell out how we make decisions (at regular church life meetings by consensus of those present). In the understandings we explain the process by which a person becomes a member of the church. We list the responsibilities of shepherds, who are the leaders of each house church. Some of these things may change. We might decide that shepherds should be responsible only for pastoral care and not administration, for example. Putting such matters into the understandings makes it clearer that these ways of doing things make life in the church better for us, but they don't take on the same importance as the ultimate statements of the covenant.

Is it really necessary to write down all these specifics? Yes. We don't live our lives totally on the abstract plane, in the lofty statements about ultimate commitment. We live as Christians in the everyday grind that needs structures to organize it, that deals with the concrete and the specific.

The other reason for writing down the understandings is to allow us to hold each other accountable to them. On paper, these guides for living are not subject to our selective memories. Written understandings can also be a quick introduction to the church for newcomers.

A clear covenant can save us from anarchy or aimless wandering—or what sociologist Benjamin Zablocki has called the "tyranny of the least committed." Without clear understandings and some way to hold each other to them, any group can fall to operating according to the standards of the least committed, and the least committed gradually drive out the most committed.

Zablocki has told the story of a rural commune which operated without covenant or leadership structures and without requirements for membership. The original members spent considerable effort constructing buildings in the wilderness. But those people who came after the buildings were built had less commitment to the group and to maintaining the buildings. Eventually, the original members, frustrated, all moved away to start another commune elsewhere.[1]

The same process can happen in house churches. Falling to the level of the least common denominator is to groups like gravity is to objects on earth; it is an inevitable, natural process *unless* there are structures to keep it from happening. Just as the joists and floorboards of my house keep me from falling from the second story and keep my feet twelve feet above the ground, so the structures of the covenant and understandings can keep house churches encouraging each other toward greater commitment to Christ and the church. Clear goals, structures, and accountability within the context of mutual caring keep us moving toward becoming the people we have covenanted to be.

Writing a Covenant

The creation of a covenant can be as important as the finished product in the life of a new church. The process is seldom short or simple, but it can help the members to get to know each other better, to understand each other better, to build a sense of togetherness, and to practice skills in conflict management.

The covenanting process of the Grain of Wheat Church-Community in Winnipeg, Manitoba, illustrates well the joy and struggle of becoming the church. Spencer Estabrooks, a servant-leader in the church-community in Winnipeg, relates the process:

> We began worshipping and meeting together as a core group in September, 1981, with a view to moving towards covenant, a process which we envisioned would take six months to a year. While others soon came to share in our worship, we closed membership in the covenanting group until the covenant was completed.

> Though we had many struggles and some crises ahead of us, a number of factors augured well for coming to agreement on a covenant. Among us, we had considerable community experience and theological or pastoral training. There was also a high degree of commitment born out of years of searching and working toward community. (The move to a common neighborhood in itself indicated a high level of commitment, with all participants changing location and many leaving jobs and family contacts.) We agreed on the need for a covenant to clarify the common understanding of our life together as a local church. Also we saw it would give us a solid base, like a marriage covenant, within which to work out the difficulties which would inevitably arise. We had the added advantage that some had even been through covenanting processes on previous occasions.

Despite a sometimes almost unmanageable diversity of backgrounds, convictions, and outlooks, we had significant things in common. We shared a conviction of the call to live close together in order to love one another as the body of Christ. We also shared the belief that family, jobs, finance, and our whole way of life were to be understood within the priority of being the church and seeking God's kingdom. We also had a common commitment to nonviolence as Christ's way for us to follow. Finally, we had the benefit of advice from Virgil Vogt, a senior elder from Reba Place, during two pastoral visits which he made to us.

As we began to build our life together we soon saw that more "dying" was needed, not just in moving to Winnipeg, but in our ongoing life. Decision making was often slow and arduous as we sought to be free to work for unity. Coming to agreement as a body was seldom possible without many difficult one-to-one sessions trying to understand, confront, and be reconciled one to one.

Early in 1982 we set up a small task force to give direction to our covenanting process. At a community retreat in February this task force presented its preliminary work. First was a statement of what we could wholeheartedly affirm as already being shared. This was simple but extremely important. We needed to be reminded that we had a common foundation of love and commitment to Christ, on the basis of which we were now considering our differences. A second result of the task force's report was the formation of small (four-person) sharing groups to work at the covenanting process. We were counseled by some from the beginning that covenanting was not something which only appeared in a written document, but that it needed to take place in relationships as we were knit together through acts of generosity and love, listening and confrontation.

Altogether, we had eight sessions in these small groups. The first session was a sharing of the autobiographies of those in our small group. These autobiographies were eventually read by everyone in the core group. In the second session we shared honestly about our experiences concerning Father, Jesus, and Spirit. In the third we learned of what we had or had not experienced of forgiveness, what that meant to us, and what things remained unresolved from our past. Sessions four and five dealt with what we understood the call to discipleship to involve in practical terms. Session six covered our life together—spiritual gifts, decision making, accountability, etc. The seventh dealt with relationships to other Christians. In the eighth session we talked about the relationship of the church to the world.

In many of these sessions the object was not to discuss, but to *hear* where each person was coming from, and what visions or unresolved past experiences each was bringing with them into community. Questions were provided by the covenant task force to help people prepare for and focus this sharing.

Toward the end of our eight sessions in small groups, we responded in a general meeting to an initial written covenant prepared on the basis of reports from the small group sharing and discussion by the covenant task force members and our servant-leaders. (One of the covenant task force members had been assigned to each small group.) A number of revisions of the proposed covenant were made. At a retreat in June we continued to seek unity through small group sharing and general discussions. A number of principles for understanding covenant were clarified before or at this retreat.

First, we saw the covenant not as a doctrinal statement, but as spelling out our theological beliefs hand in hand with the practical implications for our life. Secondly, the covenant was not meant to be an exhaustive statement, but one which laid the groundwork on which we could continue to discern God's will for our lives and on which we could live together in love.

Thirdly, we acknowledged that, while we called this statement a covenant, there is only one covenant, made by God through Jesus with those who enter into it. We acknowledged that God, not we, sets the terms of this covenant. Our "covenant," then, is our response to God's covenant and our attempt to express our understanding of that covenant and its implications. Our covenant may therefore change.

Finally our covenant came to be understood as inclusive. We were all declaring by word and action our commitment to Jesus Christ and our subjection to the Spirit speaking in Scripture and through one another, and we would go as far as we could in declaring what we held in common. Any further definition would have to come about by the Spirit granting us oneness of mind as we were changed by the Spirit in our life together.

The final step in our covenanting process was a daylong retreat in July, when all twenty adults who began the covenanting process celebrated and entered into covenant with one another under God. Everyone contributed to the celebration. We all brought an ingredient for a "community" soup to symbolize our unity. It was delicious! We all participated in the "dance of the new creation," inviting one another to join in following Jesus. And we had a time of sharing what we appreciated in one another around communion. We had a hard time bringing the evening to a close.

Sunday was the children's time to be brought into the celebration with a procession through the streets to our meeting place singing, "We will sing a song unto the Lord." Worship was centered on the children, and we gathered for a gala picnic in the park afterwards.

There are now nearly twice our original number meeting with us, and we continue to rejoice at what God is doing among us.

Only God can build the church, and each time God does, it is a miracle. We know from experience.[2]

Living in the Covenant

Once written and signed, covenants are not to be laid aside. One of the ways Mennonite Church of the Servant keeps the idea of covenant alive is by *singing* the covenant. One of our members set our covenant to music early in our history, and we have enjoyed using it in worship at various times throughout the year. Other congregations use their covenant as a unison reading in worship.

Another way to keep the covenant alive (and keep membership rolls honest) is annual renewal of the covenant by all members. Each year during Lent, we begin the process of covenant renewal. In each house church, all who wish to recovenant, or to covenant with the church for the first time, share spiritual pilgrimages with each other. Then on the Thursday before Easter, the whole church meets for an agape meal, and all those accepted by their house churches sign the covenant.

The service is solemn because Maundy Thursday reminds us of the seriousness of Jesus' commitment to God's way, that took Jesus to the cross, and may also take us there. But the worship and the meal are also celebrative because we welcome new people into the church and are strengthened by the recovenanting of previous members. In the covenanting service we celebrate our life together for Jesus' sake.

Some Sample Covenants
Cedar Community Mennonite Church, Cedar Falls, Iowa
Confession of Faith, Based on 1 John 4

As Christian believers, we claim Jesus Christ as our Lord. God's love, revealed in Jesus by the power of the Holy Spirit, is central to our faith. That love is expressed to and through us as we journey together in this world.

"This is love: not that we loved God, but that he loved us and sent his Son as an atoning sacrifice for our sins. Dear friends, since God so loved us, we ought to love one another. No one has ever seen God; but if we love each other, God lives in us and his love is made complete in us. We know that we live in him and he in us, because he has given us of his Spirit" (1 John 4:10-13, NIV).

We commit ourselves to expressing God's love in the following ways:

We love God as creator and sustainer of life. We respond with praise, adoration, worship, and obedience. "We love because he first loved us" (v. 19).

We love each other as sisters and brothers in Christ. We respond by: sharing life together as disciples following after Jesus, giving freely of ourselves to one another. "Dear friends, let us love one another, for love comes from God" (v. 7).

We love all people as children of God, friends as well as enemies. We respond in service and mission to the world in the reconciling power of God. "Whoever loves God must also love his neighbor" (v. 21).

Understandings

The above affirmations of faith are considered unchanging. However, we expect our understandings of faithful obedience to be tested and adjusted. As we grow toward the fullness of Christ, we want to be open to new insights as we study and search the Scriptures together. As members of the Cedar Community Mennonite Church, we believe the following understandings are ways to express in our lives the lordship of Jesus.

1. Active participation in worship services and "Life Together" meetings is expected.

2. Close personal relationships with fellow believers are essential to the Christian life. We encourage participation in a small group of the church.

3. We see ourselves as mutually accountable to both give and receive counsel in the body of believers (Matt. 18:15-20).

4. We commit ourselves to be peacemakers and reconcilers in human conflict.

5. As caretakers of God-given gifts and material goods, we commit these resources for use in ways consistent with our faith.

6. We recognize children as gifts of God, cherished individuals with rights and privileges in our congregational life. We seek to model the way of faith in Jesus so that children may freely choose to follow him.

7. We welcome as associate members those persons who have their primary commitment in another congregation, but still want to identify with and support CCMC. Expectations for the associate relationship will be worked out in writing with each associate member.

8. Our covenant commitment, both confession of faith and understandings, will be reviewed and renewed annually.

Covenant of Mennonite Church of the Servant,
Wichita, Kansas
We commit ourselves to following Jesus Christ,
    through whom God has made friends with the world
        and in whom we continue the work of reconciliation.

We commit ourselves to each other, the church,
    to love our brothers and sisters in God's family,
        sharing our decisions, our talents, our time, and our
        possessions.

We commit ourselves to caring for the world,
to bringing good news to the poor and setting free the
   oppressed,
      to proclaiming Jesus the Servant as Liberator and Lord.

We commit ourselves to the way of the cross,
   to a life of simplicity and prayer;
      in this is our joy, peace, and new life.

(Understandings include an explanation of certain phrases of
the covenant, definition of membership, a description of group
life, and a description of leadership roles.)

Fellowship of Joy, Akron, Ohio
I will:

1. Give an initial full financial disclosure and then discuss
with the group new purchases or financial commitments.

2. Give a list of present time and schedule commitments and
discuss how these relate to the life of the fellowship.

3. Discuss with the fellowship potential vocational changes.

4. Have an attitude of willing availability to helping each
other in practical ways.

5. Receive counsel from and give counsel to the fellowship.

6. Share personal and interpersonal problems that affect my
relationship with God or the fellowship.

The Assembly, Goshen, Indiana

1. In covenanting together, we affirm that Jesus Christ is
Lord—acknowledged Lord of the church and unrecognized
Lord of the world. We gratefully acknowledge him as *our*
Lord.

2. We accept responsibility for each other as God's people in

this place and commit ourselves to building up the body of Christ as our gifts are discerned and the Spirit enables.

3. We commit ourselves to help each other to find and faithfully obey his mandate in carrying out God's mission of "uniting all things in him."

Understandings: We believe that accepting Christ as Lord and guide in all the decisions and activities of life in this time and context involve the following:

1. Active participation in a small group, in members' meetings, and in the larger Sunday morning assembly.

2. Recognition of our need to give and receive counsel with other congregations and believers in the Mennonite church and in the larger Christian church.

3. Welcoming with love and respect visitors and interested persons who attend regularly. We want to grant them the freedom necessary for real searching and integrity in decision.

4. Exercising compassionate stewardship in the use of our resources—money, time, and talents. This includes the contribution of 1 percent of our gross annual income for grassroots needs and development in the third world.

5. Living as those whom Christ calls to be peacemakers in all areas of life. We commit ourselves to reconciliation in situations of brokenness and oppression, conscientious objection to military service, and the use of economic resources in a way consistent with Jesus' nonresistant love. The congregation pledges support to members refusing draft registration and war tax payment.

We recognize that there are great differences in the belief and practice of Christians and churches in these matters. In committing ourselves to the above understandings, we also express our openness to study and search with individuals and bodies of believers who differ in their understandings of the meaning of Christ's lordship. We want continually to test our understandings against all available information concerning the life and teachings of Jesus and the experiences of God's people in order that our beliefs and practices may represent, not private or extra-Christian understandings, but faithful expressions of what it means to be Christian in today's world.

Reflection and Action

1. For what would you like to be held accountable in the church? Make a list of the goals toward which you would like to be moving. Which of these things would be appropriate to include in a covenant for the whole church?

2. House churches' covenants often include faith statements, moral guidelines, and a description of organizational structures. What are we saying when we include doctrine, ethics, and polity in one document? The law of Moses has this same combination of concern for belief, morality, and ritual structures. Can you find all these elements in the apostle Paul's letters? Study 1 Corinthians, for example, to find doctrine (belief statements), moral expectations, and structures for orderly worship.

3. A covenant does not need to say everything. It does need to include the church's common assumptions, the essentials of their faith, and the basic structures for their life together. What are the things on which your group already has unity? Are there other items on which you need unity before you can be the church?

Chapter 3

Worship

"God is round," one of my teachers at seminary often said. He said it with a twinkle in his eye, but he was mostly serious about his metaphor. House churches, too, must believe that God is round, for the roundness is imitated by house churches in their structures for worship. Sitting in a complete circle or in an open circle is not only a symbol for the church's life together in the image of God, but a physical structuring of relationships that helps people worship together. It is a structure that helps people use their spiritual gifts "for building up the body of Christ" (Eph. 4:12, RSV).

A circle symbolizes the ministry of each one to the other. It encourages that ministry on the part of many people, not just one. Sitting face-to-face puts us in touch with each other and ready to hear the word of God coming to us through the other—or ready to speak that word to the other. The circle releases us from the passivity which is encouraged when the congregation is divided into performers on the chancel and audience in the pews. The circle is a nonverbal message that we all are priests, that we all are participants in worship, that any of us may be led to speak the word of comfort or caution, that where two or three are gathered in the name of Christ, he is present, drawing them together in unity.

This kind of participatory worship must have been the worship toward which the house church in Corinth was aiming. Paul wrote to them so that they might have order in worship, but not to squelch the broad participation in worship already happening there. First Corinthians 14:26-33 says,

> When you come together, *each one* has a hymn, a lesson, a revelation, a tongue, or an interpretation. Let all things be done for edification. If any speak in a tongue, let there be only two or at most three, and each in turn; and let one interpret. But if there is no one to interpret, let each of them keep silence in church and speak to himself and to God. Let two or three prophets speak, and let the others weigh what is said. If a revelation is made to another sitting by, let the first be silent. For you can all prophesy one by one, so that all may learn and all be encouraged; and the spirits of prophets are subject to prophets. For God is not a God of confusion, but of peace (RSV, italics mine).

How do we include this kind of participation, "roundness," into the various elements of worship? Let us look at five emphases that can be included in house church worship.

Praise

When we praise, we say, "God, how wonderful you are because. . . ." Then we say what it is that God has done for us and for others. We celebrate our covenant with God and with each other. We acknowledge who it is who rules over the whole earth. Steve Schmidt of New Creation Fellowship in Newton, Kansas, has written:

> We need a place for praise and thanksgiving; what is inside us needs to come out! A poster which quotes Psalm 92 says it well, "Lord, you have done so much for me, no wonder I am glad!" Individually and corporately we have come to the awareness of

how much God has done for us. In many cases, God has saved our marriages; God has healed us from many painful memories and wounds of youth; God has filled up vacancies and deficits in our hearts from our lonely years; God has given us committed brothers and sisters; God has helped us forgive those who have hurt us (freeing us from resentments); God has set us free from the painfully wrong things we have done (helping us deal with our guilt); and God has put us into service for God (including knitting our gifts together into a functioning body of Christ). "O Lord, you have done so much for us, no wonder we are glad! No wonder we want to come together to worship and thank you."

We used to think that all you needed to do was to put people together—especially if they were well-meaning Christians—and they would get along fine. Our naivete about that is gone: without God we could not live together in a nondestructive way. Our sustained life together causes us to praise and thank God because we know it is a gift from God.

So one important function worship serves our church-community is to provide occasion for expression of our praise and thanksgiving.[1]

Such praise can take the form of spoken testimonies of what God has been doing in our lives. Often it seems natural to express our praise through singing. Singing is a way to praise in which almost everyone can share.

There is nothing inherently wrong with choirs, solo musicians, and so forth, but the smaller the church, the more appropriate it is for everyone to sing together.

At Mennonite Church of the Servant, we do a lot of singing, sometimes songs chosen by the worship leader, sometimes songs suggested from the group. We use various portable instruments for accompaniment: guitars, Autoharps, recorder, violin. One reason for this is practical. When house churches or the Gathering (of all the house churches) meet for worship, there is usually no piano or organ. The instruments we use have to be portable. The other benefit is that small, hand-held instruments allow the players to be part of the circle of worship rather than sitting outside the circle or with their backs turned to it.

Prayer

Prayer is our communication with God. To define prayer in that way means that prayer, like any other kind of communication, can be verbal or nonverbal. At times, we include periods of silence in our worship together. During this time, we can speak our personal, silent prayers to God, but more important, we can allow God to speak to us. We sit comfortably, close our eyes, relax our muscles, and open ourselves first to the experience of God's presence and then to listening to what God wants to communicate to us.

At other times, we speak our prayers. One form for praying which allows many people to participate is what is called in the high church liturgies the "prayers of the people." Many worshipers offer their prayer concerns to the church, and after each concern, the congregation responds, "Lord, hear our prayer."

Another form for praying is the "bidding" prayer. The worship leader suggests a topic or concern for prayer and after each concern leaves a period in which each person may make his or her own prayers. *The Book of Common Prayer*, for example, suggests, "Guide the people of this land, and of all nations, in the ways of justice and peace; that we may honor one another and serve the common good." *Silence*.

"Give us all a reverence for earth as your own creation, that we may use its resources rightly in the service of others and to your honor and glory." *Silence*, etc.

Or we may wish to allow people to speak prayers out of the silence as they are led to do so.

Prayers of confession may occasionally be appropriate in corporate worship. The best time and place for confession of wrongs done to another person is soon after the wrong is done or certainly before the service of worship. In the words of Matthew 5:23-24: "So if you are offering your gift at the altar, and there remember that your brother has something against you, leave your gift there before the altar and go, first be reconciled to your brother, and then come and offer your gift" (RSV). Even some of the liturgical churches are suggesting moving confession out of the regular worship service to the beginning of the liturgy or as a separate service.

Remembrance

In worship we not only celebrate what God is doing for us now, we remember what God has done for our forebears in the faith. In the Bible, especially, we are reminded of the faith journeys of men and women who were friends of God: Abraham and Sarah, who journeyed to a distant land away from kindred because they believed God would keep an almost impossible promise; Moses, Miriam, and Aaron, who welded a group of slaves into a nation of Yahweh and led them from oppression to freedom; the prophets, who spoke the Word the people did not want to hear; Priscilla and Aquila, who taught and evangelized. In the Bible, we particularly learn about Jesus, whose faith journey through cross and resurrection we take as our ultimate guide. In remembering the history of the church since biblical times, we are reminded of Francis, Teresa, Peter Chelcicky, Martin Luther King, Jr., and Dorothy Day, who let God work in their lives.

In the remembering we are freed from our provincialism. We can see outside our own time and place to God's work in human lives in many other times and places. We forge the link between us and the friends of God throughout the centuries. We both affirm the commonness of our faith journey with them and we learn from them.

It is important to be in touch with the present. It is important to discern God's will for today and tomorrow. But we do those things best when we do not cut ourselves off from the church's past.

In the house church, we not only tell our stories, we tell The Story. It is the story of God's interaction with humanity throughout history, but especially God's action in history through Jesus, and because of Jesus, our own relationship with God. We tell the story by reading Scripture, by telling general church history and our own congregation's history. We tell how God has been at work in our own lives. We tell the story formally in readings, teaching, and drama. We tell it informally in discussion and in times of praise and prayer.

Often the church's worship has focused on the abstract—the rational ideas condensed from Scripture, the moral principles. But abstract ideas and principles alone rob us of the power of the story to touch us in a new way and to transform our lives into a more Christlike shape. As we are reminded of the story, we connect it with our stories.

Teaching

We will examine teaching in the house church in greater detail in Chapter 4. But teaching in worship deserves some comment at this point. In worship we not only remind each other of God's Word in the past, we come expecting to hear God's word for the present. We hear that word in worship through each other, through the exercise of the gifts we have for each other, to build up the body of Christ. In the house church we look at the Scripture, at our own lives, at the condition of the world, and together interpret the word of God for today. Ephesians 4:11-16 notes that some were apostles, those who had had the direct experience of Jesus and were sent out to tell about that. Some were teachers, those who handed down the tradition and interpreted it. Some were evangelists, telling the good news to people outside the church. Some were pastors, looking after the needs of those within the church. But all were parts of a body, joined and knit together and building itself in love. All these different people with different gifts sharing with each other and providing different perspectives are needed to build up the body of Christ so that all can find unity of the faith and knowledge of the Son of God.

In the smallness of the house church there is no need for a steady diet of monologue sermons. Smallness, in fact, encourages the mutual sharing of gifts as we interpret the Word of God. In a smaller house church, all may have studied a particular Scripture passage or other topic in preparation for the meeting. One person may lead the discussion while all share equally in discerning the meaning of God's Word. In a larger group, such as several house churches meeting together, one person may have done special study on the passage and may give a teaching to the rest of the group, followed by group discussion, questions, personal journaling, or some other way of involving all the worshipers in the teaching and learning process. Some members of the church may have had more training in biblical studies, and that is a gift for the church which should be affirmed. Others have gifts of compassion or faith, which are of equal value in discerning the meaning of Scripture for ourselves and each other.

Commitment

In worship we also celebrate our commitment to God and to the church. We celebrate our covenant as a church each time we sign the covenant to renew our commitment to each other for the coming year. We celebrate persons' new commitments to Christ and the church through baptism.

We also express our Christian commitment through eating the Lord's Supper together. In the Old Testament, covenants were celebrated with a common meal, such as Moses and the elders' meal on Mount Sinai. In the New Testament, most of what we know about how the early church celebrated the Lord's Supper, first known simply as "the breaking of the bread," comes from the book of Acts and from 1 Corinthians 10-11.

In Acts 2:42, 46, the early Christians, immediately after Pentecost, broke bread daily in their homes, together with listening to the apostles' teaching, sharing possessions, and participating in the prayers together. Perhaps this common meal was one of the ways of providing for the needs of the poorer members. In Acts 20:7-12, the church in Troas broke bread together in a home, the meal being preceded by a very long teaching!

Since the New Testament church met in homes, we have no reason to expect that the Lord's Supper would be celebrated any place else. Whether we see the Lord's Supper growing out of the Jewish Passover tradition or growing out of Jesus' everyday table fellowship with his disciples (and with tax collectors and sinners), the home was still the location for these meals.

One of our problems in feeling comfortable with the Lord's Supper in the home may be the development of the Lord's Supper by the later church from a full meal to a symbolic one—at its extreme, a crumb of bread and a sip of wine. In the first-century church, however, the Lord's Supper was a full meal. Jesus' Last Supper with his disciples was a full meal, and the early church continued to commemorate that occasion with a full meal. A number of apostolic sources mention food other than bread and wine. Early Christian art showed fish as a eucharistic symbol. Elsewhere are mentioned meals that consisted of all sorts of meat, fish, bread, vegetables, fruit, and a drink.

The problem with the Corinthian church (see 1 Cor. 11:17-34) was not that they were making the Lord's Supper into a full meal when they should not have, but that some people were eating up all the food and drinking all the wine before the last folks arrived. William Orr and James Walther in the Anchor Bible commentary on 1 Corinthians have noted that "Paul's instruction begins with his chagrin, not that the Corinthians are profaning a holy rite, but that they are fragmenting a holy society."[2] To create division in the church is to profane the body of Christ. Paul's instruction for the hungry to eat at home first was so that they would not then be tempted to eat all the food at the common meal and leave none for the latecomers.

The meal was intended to symbolize the unity of the body of Christ. Robert Banks has written in *Paul's Idea of Community*.

> The meal that they shared together not only reminded the members of their relationship with Christ and one another but actually deepened it, much as participation in a common meal by a family or group not only symbolizes but really cements the bond between them. This explains why Paul does not direct his criticisms against the attitudes of people to the elements of bread and wine, or the quality of their individual relationships to God, but rather against their attitudes and behaviour *towards one another*.[3]

The meal was thus a symbol of their commitment to each other as well as to the death-and-resurrection way of Jesus. As brothers and sisters in God's family, they saw the common meal as part of the glue that continued to bind them together.

What most closely resembles the common meal of the early church in our house churches is our frequent potluck dinners.

They are one of the ways that we build and celebrate relationships within the house church. Perhaps we could be more intentional about the spiritual nature of our potluck dinners and other common meals. Instead of seeing their function as "just" fellowship, we can see them as continuing the table fellowship of Jesus and the common meals of the early church. These meals can be an opportunity for frequent renewal of our covenant with God and with each other. They can function both as the expression of, and the creation of, the unity of the body of Christ.

At Mennonite Church of the Servant we have sometimes said the prayers over the bread before the common meal and shared the cup after the meal together with a simple liturgy. Other times we have had a simpler communion meal with only bread and the cup. In either style of the Lord's Supper we declare our being in relationship with God and with the church. Just as biological families build up their relationships through eating together, so the family of God builds relationships through the act of eating together.

Our commitment as Christians, however, is not only to inner spiritual growth and to each other in the church, but also to the well-being, the shalom, of the world. In our teaching, in our prayers, in our commissionings, in our encouragements of each other, worship should include a concern that God's love be made known among all peoples.

Being Intentional About Worship

In all these elements of worship—praise, prayer, remembering, teaching, and commitment—we need a sense of order or structure or intentionality. Order does not need to mean formality. Nor does it require that we eliminate all spontaneity from our worship. I have been a part of Catholic masses where many of the words spoken were those required by the liturgy, yet a sense of warmth and spontaneity was present in the kiss of peace before communion and in the shared prayers offered by the worshipers.

What is necessary no matter what the size of the worshiping group or its liturgical commitments (or lack thereof) is intentionality—knowing what it is that we want to do during worship. In a small house church, this may mean deciding on a simple order of worship: first we will sing, then we will study, then we will share what the last week has been like for us, then we will pray. Often this will mean designating someone as worship leader, someone who can say, "Let's have one more song and then go on to our study." My experience is that even minimal structure reduces the tension level in the room. It allows participants to focus on what is being said or sung, rather than worrying about what will happen next or whether they will have a chance to pray about their concerns.

Even if the house church has chosen an unprogrammed style of worship, it is necessary to be intentional about saying, "Today we are having an unprogrammed worship." This in itself is a structure that lets people know that periods of silence are okay and that each person is responsible for listening to the Spirit speaking in him or her and sharing that with the church if led to do so.

House church structures for worship may be open and allow for much spontaneity, but some kind of structure is necessary, or else what was to have been a time of worship may collapse into a time of unfocused conversation (or even separate conversations in different corners of the room)!

A good worship leader for a house church is one who keeps the church focused on God's actions and our responses and feels authorized by the group to do what it has said it wants to do in worship.

I have also found it helpful to be intentional about involving the whole person in worship, not just the intellect. Holistic worship involves not only discussion of concepts, but expression of feelings, the touch that says, "I care," the music that expresses the joy or sorrow that words alone cannot, the common meal with its tastes and smells, the body movements of procession or dance, drama which tells the story in the new way, or the banner that draws our attention visually. While the house church may not be able to make music with large choirs and pipe organs or to meet the eye with high arches, vaults, and stained-glass windows, the house church is better suited to holistic worship than the cathedral. In the house church, worshipers can involve their whole selves, not just their listening selves, but their speaking, touching, doing selves in worship which can touch their deepest needs and help them touch others' lives. In such worship "in the round," we move toward becoming whole.

Reflection and Action

1. Think of a worship service in the past two years that spoke to your deepest self. What did the worship service include? What was it that touched you deeply? How were you involved in the service?

2. How can you better involve your whole self in worship through praise? prayer? remembrance, or telling the story? teaching, or interpreting the word of God for today? commitment?

3. Make two columns on a page. At the top of one write "eight people," and at the top of the other column write, "one hundred eighty people." List under each column the kinds of worship experiences that happen best in each size group. Are there some kinds of worship experiences that seem to fit both sizes of group? Are there some kinds that need a group of in-between size, say, fifty people?

Chapter 4

Teaching and Learning

The assumption of all teaching and learning is that people are in process. That is true in the house church as much as in any other educational setting. Faith is a commitment to a journey, the process of moving closer to God. The prophets saw Israel's time of greatest faithfulness to God as the wilderness journey. Psalm 25 asks, "Make me to know thy ways, O Lord; teach me thy paths. Lead me in thy truth and teach me, for thou art the God of my salvation; for thee I wait all the day long" (vv. 4-5, RSV). Jesus invited his disciples to "follow me." The early Christians were called followers of the way.

Faith as a journey implies that all of us are learners together. None of us has arrived. We all are in the process of learning what to do and how to be better followers of Jesus. We look to Jesus, our ultimate Guide, for instruction on how to follow, how to head in the right direction and be saved from aimless wandering. We need to be saved from that kind of floating which has no aims, no plans, no sense of satisfaction. Jesus' way of ministry, death, and resurrection gives meaning to our suffering and helps us be with others who are suffering.

Directions for the Journey
Where do we go to find directions for our faith journey?

Scripture. In the Bible we find stories of divine initiative and human response. We find the record of the faith journeys of many friends of God, from Abraham and Sarah to the suffering churches in the Revelation of John. We read of the faith journey of a covenant people who moved from oppression in Egypt to covenant with God in the wilderness to struggle in the Promised Land.

We read the faith journeys of first-century house churches in Corinth who struggled with church discipline, order in worship, and giving priority to love. We learn especially of Jesus, who is the Way, and whose way we commit ourselves to follow. So we go to the Bible as our basic source of teaching.

History. We also learn from the history of the church since the first century. We learn from the orthodox churches and from renewal movements. We look at how people in later centuries translated the faith journeys of the Bible. We look at the history of our own forebears in the faith to see how God was working in their lives.

Teachers. Although the three major lists of spiritual gifts, or roles, in the first-century house churches do not include all the same gifts, all three lists mention the role of teaching (Rom. 12:7; 1 Cor. 12:29; Eph. 4:11). Not everyone is equally able to teach everything. House churches find it helpful to have one or more people who are designated as teachers because of their skill in teaching and because of their ability to study the Bible and history and interpret that to others. There is a role for the teacher trained in biblical and theological studies. Such a person can open our eyes to new and serious ways of looking at the Scriptures and our world. The teacher's role is not just to give information, but to help learners discover for themselves the riches of the Bible and of other pilgrims of the faith. The best teachers do not so much put us in awe of their learning, but excite us to begin the journey of learning which they also have begun. The teacher cannot transform others' behavior. But the teacher can guide people to the place where they can have the "aha" experience for themselves and choose to walk down new paths.

The leader's method may often be that of asking questions. The idea is not to dispense information, but to guide the members of the church in the process of discovering for themselves what the Scripture means for them. "Some will have extensive background in biblical study. Others will have next to none," Walter Wink has written in *Transforming Bible Study: A Leader's Guide.* "Nevertheless we are all equals before the text, for in regard to our own experience we are all experts. And since it is the intersection of the text with experience which evokes insights, no one need feel disadvantaged."[1]

The present. As important as the Bible and the history of God's people are to the church, we recognize that we also learn from the present. God's revelation to humankind did not stop with Revelation 22:21. God continues to speak to us and to teach us to understand how God's way, the way of Jesus, applies to our situation. Through private prayer and meditation, we experience the presence of God and the message of the Holy Spirit, who "will teach you all things" (John 14:26). However, it is not only to individuals that the Holy Spirit speaks, but to the gathered church.

The Anabaptists of sixteenth-century Europe believed that the Bible and all revelations from the Spirit were best interpreted in the community of believers. There, private interpreatations could be tested for their consistency with God's message as it had already been revealed. Not only was the Spirit present in discerning the truth of private interpretations, but the Spirit was present in the gathered body of believers as they waited in expectation for the new word and presence of the Spirit in their midst.

Our worship gains a new sense of excitement as we come anticipating new teaching for the present as we meet for worship and study. Our gathering is more than just a collection of our individual interpretations and ideas; the whole is more than the sum of the parts. In the presence of the church, we perceive a more complete teaching of the Spirit. When we come in expectation of a new word from the Spirit, worship becomes an experience of allowing for change in ourselves and in our behavior as Christians. It is also true of teaching in worship what Henri J. M. Nouwen has written of prayer:

> Praying, therefore, means being constantly ready to let go of your certainty and to move on further than where you are now. It demands that you take to the road again and again, leaving your house and looking forward to a new land for yourself and your fellowman. This is why praying demands poverty, that is, the readiness to live a life in which you have nothing to lose so that you always begin afresh.[2]

I have found it helpful to have some time for silence in worship in order to assimilate what has been said and consider its relevance for me, but also to allow the Spirit to continue the teaching during my time of meditation.

Teaching to the Whole Person

One temptation in Bible study is to read the passage and jump directly into "what does this verse mean for me today?" The methods of historical and literary criticism have been a helpful corrective to this because they have encouraged us to look first at what that verse meant to the people who said it or did it and to the person who wrote it down. We know now that to understand a biblical passage, we need to know its context.

Nevertheless, it has been difficult to build the bridge from the historical and literary context of the passage to its relevance now for me and my church. In the end, our knowledge of the historical setting may be of no more help to us in changing our lives than undisciplined and uninformed speculation on the passage. Is there some way of combining the concern for faithfulness to the original context with concern for our faithful action today?

Walter Wink outlines one way of making this connection in his book *Transforming Bible Study*. Wink advocates using both the left and right halves of the brain in encountering Scripture. Much of our schooling teaches us to use the left side of the brain, which normally specializes in putting things in the right order, cause-and effect relationships, speech, logic, analysis, math problems, grammar, abstract thinking, and processing information in an orderly fashion. The right hemisphere of the brain handles spatial relationships, putting together the whole, and the grasping of meanings in context. It perceives shapes, sizes, textures, and colors. It is the center most active in meditation, dreaming, imaging, complex visual patterns, and the recognition of melodies. While the left side of the brain looks at the trees, the right side sees the forest.

We are our most creative when we use both sides of our brains. Wink has written:

> The case for encountering Scripture with our total selves does not rest on brain theory anyway; people have encountered Scripture thus in every age. I am simply using brain theory to suggest why such a total encounter is necessary, and to help the prospective leader understand that those exercises which are intended to evoke right hemispheric engagement with the text are not simply devices for "getting people involved," but are indispensable for the transformative process itself. Such exercises go far beyond asking what the text means for us; they "somaticize" the text—they cause the insights it fosters to be experienced as a "felt sense" within the body.[3]

So with the left brain, we look at the historical context. We analyze how a particular word is used in this passage and elsewhere in the Bible. With the right brain, we understand biblical metaphors, parables, and wordplays. We understand the whole with our right brains, after the left hemisphere has analyzed the parts. Through dialogues with characters from parables or stories, role play, painting, mime, or movement, we gain new insights into the biblical passage.

This kind of Bible study calls for a four-step process.

1. First we understand as best we can what the author of the text meant. We observe what the text says. We tell the story. Who is involved? Where? How? What is the historical background? How is this text like or different from others? What is the main emphasis of the text? What is the literary form of the passage? narrative? parable? poetry? discourse? Where else in the Bible does the main idea of this passage appear? How does this idea fit with the good news as we know it through Jesus? For a time, we step out of our time and culture and into the time and culture of the passage. What was it like then?

2. Then we use our right brains to try to live into the passage until it becomes vivid for us. If the passage is a narrative, we may try to imagine ourselves as one of the characters in the story through role playing or through dialogue in our journals. Or we may try to understand the symbols and images used in the story.

3. The third step is to apply the biblical context to ourselves. We can do this with both the left and right sides of the brain. With our analytical side, we can consult Bible commentaries. How has the text been interpreted by others? Even if the passage seems bound to its culture and not directly applicable to ours, is the process or function helpful to us? With the right side of the brain, we allow the text to move within us. "By music, movement, painting, sculpting, written dialogues, and

small-group sharing, we can allow the text to unearth that part of our personal and social existence which it calls forth to be healed, forgiven, transformed," Wink has written.[4]

4. Finally, we let the text change or convert us. We study. We respond in obedience. Then we understand the Scripture more fully as we live it out. Anabaptist reformer Hans Denck wrote, "Whoever would know Christ must follow him in life, and whoever would follow him, must know him." As we act as the Scripture asks us to act, we understand more about what the Scripture means. Then we go back to it with new insights from our action and new questions and learn more about what the Bible means for our lives.

Steps one and two can be done with a large group or a small group, but step three is best done in a group of from five to twelve, a house-church-size group. In step three, we get personally involved in the text. We understand it, not only with our intellect, but with our intuition, as we talk about how we identify with the characters in the story or as we get in touch with our feelings regarding the story.

Take the story of the prodigal son in Luke 15:11ff., for example. I learned something new about the story when I looked at the social context of the parable. Jesus told this parable to the Pharisees and scribes, who had been criticizing him for associating with tax collectors and sinners (see vv. 1 and 2). So no matter how much we may have emphasized the love of the waiting father who rejoices in the homecoming of his wayward son, the real climax of the parable is the father's response to the jealous older brother, who, like the scribes and the Pharisees, cannot understand why the good boy and the bad boy do not get equal treatment from the father.

But I learned more about the parable as I journaled a dialogue between me as the younger brother and the father. I questioned, Was it all right for me to use and celebrate the gifts

God had given me, even though others close to me were jealous of my gifts? In the process of journaling, it occurred to me that the parable says that the older son shares in all that is the father's. The older son has gifts, too. It is all right for me to accept my gifts from God, even though not everyone else likes what God has done. I need to affirm the gifts of the older brother as well. Analyzing the context of the parable gave me knowledge. Putting myself into the parable gave me understanding that could change my behavior.

Alternatives for Teaching and Learning
in the House Church

Teaching and learning in the house church are not confined to sermons or Sunday school discussions. Consider some of the alternatives:

—A formal teaching, or sermon, in the weekly worship followed immediately by discussion in groups of from three to five.

—A formal teaching integrated with a time of guided meditation or journaling on the subject of the teaching and how it affects me.

—Reading a passage of Scripture and then expressing the idea of the text in art. One Palm Sunday, Mennonite Church of the Servant divided into groups to work on the text for the day. One group wrote a song. Another group prepared a drama on the reactions of various people in the Palm Sunday story to the events of the day. Another group prepared a dance to the hymn "Ride on, Ride on in Majesty." A fourth group drew pictures and made collages.

—A Bible study using the question method. In this style, the leader's task is to ask questions, rather than to give answers. The task is not to do the discovery for people and bring it back to them, but to guide people in the process of discovering for themselves. Begin with asking, Who? What? When? Where? Why? What were the feelings of the characters in the story, if it is a narrative? What part of you is like the characters in the story?

—Using denominationally prepared adult Sunday school materials or study books, or books telling the story of congregations like Church of the Saviour in Washington, D.C.

—Teaching integrated with worship.

—Separate "issues nights" on issues in society which the church wants to address, or issues in church members' lives.

Teaching and learning in the house church mean bringing ourselves to the process of becoming better followers of Jesus. We bring all our resources. We bring any special training. We bring our personal life experiences. We bring our historical traditions. We bring the Scriptures. And we help each other move in the Godward direction in the faith journey.

Reflection and Action

Practice using your whole brain in a study of Mark 10:32-52. Do this study with your house church, or by yourself journal on the following questions:

Begin by reading Mark 10:32-52, perhaps with different people reading the parts of the disciples (and the narrative), Jesus, James and John, and Bartimaeus. How does this story open? Who is there? What are they doing? How are they feeling?

Where are they going? Where is Jesus in the group?

For what are James and John asking? Do they think they have a chance of receiving what they are asking for? (Hint: What happened in 9:28?)

What does it mean to sit at the right hand or left hand of Jesus in his glory? What is the cup that Jesus will drink? (See Mark 14:36.) What is his baptism?

What is the response of James and John? Who is it that is angry at James and John? What is Jesus' response to James and John on a feeling level? Does he condemn them? Is he angry? Does Jesus say it is wrong to want to be great in the kingdom? What is the realism that Jesus injects? How does one go about being great in the kingdom?

Where does the next scene take place? What else happened at Jericho? (See Josh. 6.) Who is there? What does it mean to call Jesus "Son of David"? How does Jesus usually refer to himself? (See vv. 33, 45.) Why would people, or the disciples, tell Bartimaeus to be quiet? What does Jesus ask him? Have we seen this question before?

How is Bartimaeus's response different from that of James and John? What was the source of Bartimaeus's faith? What was his response to healing? Was it different from the response of James and John?

What part of you is like James and John? What part of you wants to be next to Jesus in his glory, but doesn't know what you are asking? Are you able to drink the cup that Jesus drinks? What does that mean for you?

Earlier in Mark, in the story of the rich young ruler, Jesus says, "All things are possible with God." Does this help you say, "I am able"?

What part of you is like Bartimaeus, saying, "Have mercy on me"? How do you feel when you are like Bartimaeus? What do you want Jesus to do for you?

Are you willing to pay the price? What is the price for you?

Chapter 5

Children

The Sunday school has become such a standard part of the Protestant way of relating to children in the church that it is hard for many house churches to imagine other ways of nurturing children in the faith. It is on the "problem" of Sunday school that many house churches founder, as they lose families whose children are becoming of Sunday school age.

We can remind ourselves that the church existed for over seventeen centuries without the Sunday school as we know it. When the Sunday school was started in England, it was for children without parents who cared for their spiritual upbringing. There are alternative ways of educating children in the context of the church. As house churches work to create new forms of church for adults, they can also work to create new forms of church that will meet the needs of children and their parents.

The basic metaphor for the house church is family, being brothers and sisters to each other, and all living in a child-parent relationship to God. So it is appropriate that our church family include children, too. If the essence of the house church for adults is building relationships of trust and caring in which we can disciple each other in the process of following Christ, then the experience of house church for children can also be building that kind of relationship which allows for both love and discipline.

When our oldest daughter was five, there were few children in our church. But she enjoyed going to church because two or three adults took the time to seek her out, hold her, talk to her, and treat her as an important person. Now that she is eleven, she values relationships with some of the younger, single women in the church.

A house church in Cedar Falls, Iowa, has an "uncle-aunt" program in which each child in the congregation has a surrogate uncle or aunt who regularly schedules activities with that child.

These "family" members in the house church can provide children with role models for Christian living. Ruth Klaassen of the Kitchener-Waterloo (Ont.) House Churches has written:

> Within my house church the teaching, learning, meals, games, and relaxation have all been done together with adults and children. Worship was to be a time of quietness and devotion; at other times we learned to relax in the knowledge that the children were present and listening even if they held crayons or a book. The example and knowledge passed on from parents or elders to a child is more than a source of information and a skill. It helps the children to identify with the model, to become more autonomous, independent, and secure.

> Children need to experience worship and education with their parents. It is important for a child to see his or her parents pray and to see other respected adults pray, to hear adults talk of religious matters, and to know that he or she is a part of this experience. It is important for the children to know that the God of the adult world is also the God of their world and that the comprehension of God on the part of the elder is not too far from that of the child.[1]

Children in Worship

House churches can include children in at least part of their worship time. It often works best to include children in the more active times of worship, such as singing. Children like to sing, especially songs that are familiar and easily sung. Children can be participants or eager observers in drama. Simple movements to songs can encourage a child's participation. Children can offer their own prayer concerns. Older children can hand out songbooks or printed programs or light candles. Some can read Scripture. Children can help make banners for display in worship. If they are learning to play a musical instrument, they can play a special song or help accompany group singing. Children, like adults, need to be needed, not just entertained. They want to be active participants in the church, not just observers.

Our church also plans a special time in the service for children. The children come to the center of the circle and sit on the floor with an adult for a story or other special activity.

Since a variety of people in our church take turns planning for worship, we have developed some guidelines for telling children's stories:

1. Try to keep the activity to five minutes or less. Small children's attention spans are limited.

2. Make concepts concrete by focusing talk around pictures (if possible, a series of pictures is better than just one), objects, flannelboards, puppets, picture books, or acting.

3. Focus the talk at the level of understanding of the medium-aged children, try to involve the older ones as helpers, and attempt to sustain the attention of the youngest ones with interesting visual materials. But don't be distressed if you've lost the attention of the toddlers.

4. In some cases, when using a book, telling the story in your own words while showing the pictures may be more interesting

for the children than reading the book word for word. Hold the book up so that all of them can see.

5. A good story can stand on its own without the moral having to be pointed out. If you feel it is important to emphasize a key concept, prepare the chilldren for it before getting into the story by saying something like, "Be thinking about how Johnny was kind to his enemies."

6. Remember that you are talking to the children as well as to adults.

7. Let the children participate by asking them questions, accepting their comments, and so forth. But keep it moving.

After the children's story, the younger children in our church leave the worship service. Someone baby-sits the toddlers. A teacher plans structured activities for the preschoolers. However, if children remain in the worship service with the adults, it is important for the church as a whole (not just parents) to work out some guidelines on what is accepted behavior of children in worship and how adults can relate helpfully to them.

Is it all right if children walk around during the service on the edge of the circle? In the middle? How much talking or moving about is acceptable? What happens if a child is behaving inappropriately? Is it solely the parents' responsibility to handle the situation? Or do others in the church have the right or responsibility to steer the child to more appropriate activities to take the child onto their laps or remove the child from the room?

Here is the list of privileges for children developed by The Assembly, Goshen, Indiana:

—To be in the midst of the congregation, not on the sidelines.

—To wander among us during worship, being the responsibility of each of us.

—To give answers during children's time without being laughed at.

—To be called by name by each adult.

—To be a valued person in the congregation.

—To be led to faith by the Christlike love, care, and modeling of each adult.

Christian Education

Faith is more caught than taught. Parents are thus the primary teachers for children's experience with God. This means that the church needs to help parents recognize their privilege and responsibility in Christian education. This responsibility is not fulfilled by sending children to Sunday school. That solution is frequently a refusal to recognize that what goes on in the home is a hundred times more important than what happens during the forty-five to sixty minutes a week that a child may spend in a typical Sunday school class.

A better solution is to assist parents in fulfilling their natural and God-given opportunities to share their faith with their children. One way of doing this is to provide books, records, and other materials for parents. The church may want to buy some of these and give them to each family. Some materials might be kept in a central place to be checked out by a family for a certain length of time. Churches can encourage parents to give time to their children and share activities with them. Some churches have set aside a certain evening each week as family-at-home night. This generates a group feeling about the activities, even though they are done separately.

Parents can find many unprogrammed "teachable moments" in the lives of their children. These may be more important than structured time together. This seems to be the point the writer of Deuteronomy had in mind when parents were told to teach their children "when you are at home and when you are away, when you are resting and when you are working" (Deut. 6:7, TEV). The reminders the Israelites had on the doorposts of their houses and on their gates were helpful in communicating their values. If we believe that our values are more caught than taught, we need to see our lifestyle and our conversations as models for our children, even more than our public religious activities.

An extension of the principle that parents are the primary teachers of their children is the family cluster model of Christian education. In the model, two or more families, along with interested single persons or couples without children, contract to meet as a group once a week from ten to twelve weeks. They agree on a course of study, giving consideration to the interests of all participants. Margaret Sawin's book *Family Enrichment with Family Clusters* outlines this model. Building on the studies of others, she develops this idea and tells of her experiences in working in it.[2]

This model, sometimes called "intergenerational education," includes nurture, discovery, and training. Bertha Harder and Marlene Kropf in *Intergenerational Learning in the Church* have written,

> When we nurture one another, we help each other become what God calls us to be. Discovery includes all the ways we learn of God and God's activity in the world. And training, or guidance, helps us act out our discipleship in the world around us.
>
> Aside from obvious reasons such as small church size or a desire for variety, why might we turn to intergenerational education? The most important reason is that our faith is best shared in a lifelike setting. Intergenerational education, with its mix of all kinds and ages of people, provides a setting where we can experience the richness of a variety of faith journeys and be stimulated to new growth.[3]

In order for intergenerational education to reach a broad age range, it will be active and experiential, and it will have a relational style. Communicating with both first-graders and senior citizens means we cannot rely on words alone or abstract concepts to teach. We will use experiences that will allow us to touch, see, taste, and smell. Instead of only talking about the parable of the leaven, we make bread dough and watch it rise. Instead of only discussing the story of Peter's release from prison, we act it out. We make a human "wall of Jericho" and fall down as the trumpets blow. We not only discuss suffering, but make a collage of magazine pictures illustrating human suffering. Doing as well as talking allows all ages to participate in the learning experience, and each person may be learning at different levels.

A relational style means that people are more important than finishing the lesson. Listening to each other is more important than having a polished drama. This style recognizes that it does not matter so much whether all of the teacher's knowledge is shared with the class. It does matter that people are growing in their abilities to be Christlike, that they are finding healing and forgiveness for the wounds of the past, that they are seeking and finding direction in their lives, and that the class is an environment where people can have the freedom to be real and vulnerable and even fail.

A variety of resources for intergenerational education or family clusters is available. (See the bibliography, *More Resources for House Churches*, at the back of the book.) Or you can take traditional Sunday school material for grade-school-age children and adapt it for intergenerational use.

Intergenerational education is a good option for including a wide range of ages, but it usually does not work very well with preschool children. Preschoolers ask for and need a lot of adult attention in their activities and have shorter attention spans. If materials are kept at a level that preschoolers can understand, it is hard to keep up youth or adult interest. So a separate class for preschoolers (perhaps preschoolers from several house churches) may meet the needs of both the preschoolers and the older learners in the church. What is important is that each learner feel valued and stimulated for further Christian growth.

Youth can participate well in intergenerational education, but another option for high-school-age youth is mentoring. This involves the matching of one young person with one adult mentor from the congregation (chosen in consultation with the youth, parents, and mentor). The goal of the relationship is that the mentor be a friend and guide to the youth in the process of deciding about faith, values, vocation, lifestyle, and relationship. In some congregations youth choose a mentor when they turn twelve years old. Then the young person and mentor plan regular activities together—recreation as well as structured discussion times. In other congregations, the relationship begins when the youth enters senior high school. If there is more than one youth in the congregation, there can be occasional meetings of all youth and their mentors. In another congregation, a young person becomes an apprentice to an adult who is serving the congregation in a special role.

The advantage of this youth-adult pairing is that, during a time when youth may be less receptive to advice from their parents, youth have contact with adults in the church who care about them. And youth have opportunities to test out participation in the church and be with adults for whom the church is important. Through mentoring you can be far more involved in the church than traditional peer-youth-group activities may allow.

The house church that seeks wholeness will also value children and youth and seek to support them and disciple them into the family of God as carefully as the church does for adults.

Reflection and Action

1. This chapter lists several alternatives for meeting the needs of children and youth in the house church:

—Being a friend to a child.

—Involving children in worship.

—Letting children observe adults involved in the church.

—Providing Christian education resources for families to use at home.

—Planning intergenerational classes for school-age children and up.

—Planning separate preschool classes.

—Being a mentor to youth.

What other alternatives could you list? One congregation of house churches takes its youth on regular all-weekend retreats in lieu of every-Sunday-morning Sunday school.

2. Make your own list of the rights of the child in the church. How should adults relate to children? What behavior is expected of children? Of youth?

Chapter 6

Sharing

We live in an individualistic culture that values doing things on our own and not needing anyone else's help. Our culture encourages us, especially men, to keep feelings to ourselves. More and more people live alone and eat alone. Nuclear families are hundreds or thousands of miles from grandparents and other relatives. Families are broken by divorce and separation. For those looking for a place to belong, the church becomes family. We find that sense of family best in a family-size group: the house church.

A sense of family develops in a house church as we share the kinds of things that families share—food, time, help, love, money, decision—in short, ourselves. As we share with each other, we develop a sense of closeness and of unity in the Spirit. As we disclose who we are, where we have been, and where we want to be going, and listen gently to others do the same, we become family.

Becoming Family

The house church becomes family as we provide an opportunity to share the events of the week—what has made us happy, what has made us sad. Our house church usually allows about thirty minutes for this, followed by, or including, prayer that lifts up all these concerns to God. We do not force anyone to share. Going around the circle may not always be helpful. We allow people to share at the level at which they feel comfortable.

The house church becomes family as we stand with people in times of crisis. Sometimes one person may need most of the house church's meeting time for talking about crisis agenda. So we listen and stand with the victim of assault, or the unemployed person, or the person whose apartment has burned, or the one whose family is in conflict, or the one who is sick.

We become family as we play together. Our church has had swimming parties, bowling parties, a goat roast at the lake, retreats at a nearby church camp twice a year, volleyball nights, and campouts. A lot of what goes on in the church is social. We provide many opportunities for people to get together and talk. House churches have frequent potluck dinners. The whole church has a potluck dinner once a month. Those of us who live in the same neighborhood have two more potluck dinners a month. Some get together for breakfast every Tuesday morning at a neighborhood restaurant. If the church is to be family, all these activities help build family relationships.

We become family as we touch each other. It may be more appropriate to hold the hand of someone overcome with grief than to talk. After our *agape* meals, we share the kiss of peace or a "holy hug" as a way of giving and receiving affirmation. Sometimes holding hands in a circle as we pray is a way of demonstrating our unity in the Spirit.

We become family as we live close to each other. In Mennonite Church of the Servant, about half the members live within a few blocks of each other. That gives opportunity for contact at other times besides regular meeting times. Informal sharing times add to our sense of closeness. In Evanston, Illinois, a house church bought a six-unit apartment building, where some of its members live. Other members live near there. The whole church gatherings are in the basement. Intentional communities have shared households with both marrieds and singles.

The house church develops closer relationships as we share spiritual discoveries and doubts with each other. We come together without pretending that we have all the answers and have always had them. We draw close to each other as we share what we are really thinking, not just what we think we ought to about the issues of ultimate concern. We come to the church at whatever place we are in our spiritual journeys. If we find that our journey is taken seriously and not despised, then we are free to share even more of our journey with others in the house church.

We become closer to each other as we work together. The work may be as simple as helping someone to move to a new house. Or the work may be as demanding as developing and carrying out a common mission. People in house churches share child care or help each other shingle a roof.

We become family as we experience conflict with each other. The process of sharing our differences and facing the problems we have with each other can actually bring us close together. We can gain a new appreciation for the variety of gifts present in the church. We can celebrate that we have expressed our differences and we are still together, committed to Christ's church. Hiding our differences, on the other hand, can create distance as we gradually increase the number of sub jects about which we cannot talk to each other.

The house church becomes family as we make decisions together. As we struggle with tough decisions, the major ideas and relationships that hold us together become more evident. We gain new appreciation for each other, and we may glimpse a new vision of what we may become together. We also grow closer as we share major personal decisions, whether to marry, whether to change jobs, how to deal with strained relationships.

We become family as we share our money and possessions with each other. Money and property are powerful symbols, and how we use them shows what is important to us. Is money only for private use? Is it shared within the church? Is it shared with others in need? During the seven years I lived in a household with a common treasury, I came to realize that sharing money, in itself, was not a problem for me. But sharing money implied that I would share many other areas of my life: decisions on what kind of food I ate, emotional support, priorities. Where my treasure was, there was my heart also. The structure of the common treasury provides greater equality and security, but requires more time spent in decision-making about finances.

In some churches, economic sharing happens spontaneously, whenever the need arises. People borrow lawn mowers, books, typewriters, cars. But without specific structures for sharing, some people in need in the church may be hesitant to ask for money. A simple structure for economic sharing is the mutual aid fund. The church budget may have a specific amount written in each year, or the congregation may have a special fund into which members may contribute as the need arises. Then persons in need can know to whom to go to ask for money from the fund.

At Pilgrims Mennonite Church, Akron, Pennsylvania, special collections are taken for emergency or one-time needs, and people are directed to give what they feel is appropriate. The church also supports individuals in financial need with monthly stipends as practical. The congregation pays for Mennonite Mutual Aid, a health care program, in part or whole, depending on a family's income.

Covenant Mennonite Church, Hesston, Kansas, has made

no-interest student loans. In the London (United Kingdom) Mennonite Fellowship, a koinonia fund is supplied from 10 percent of the offerings to help people in the fellowship who are in need.

Another structure for sharing is to recommend a standard of living for all members, perhaps the salary given to denominational missionaries. Any money earned above that amount would go to the congregation, and some of this could be used to make more equal the incomes of those making less than the guidelines.

Self-Disclosure

Becoming family is related to self-disclosure. We become closer to others, and we are more likely to get our needs met and meet others needs, when we share ourselves with them. That is precisely what attracts many people to the house church—and what repels others. Sharing ourselves with others is a risk. We may spill out ourselves and find that others trample on what we thought was precious. We make ourselves vulnerable, and we may get hurt.

Em Griffin in *Getting Together: a Guide for Groups*[1] has suggested that the question of whether to reveal personal history, private thoughts, and hidden emotions is not one of either-or. Rather, it is a question of appropriateness. It makes a difference *who* is the recipient of our openness. Most of our relationships are governed by roles. Intimate self-disclosure needs to be reserved for the few. We have only so much time. We should choose people we trust, people who are slow to judge, members of a house church who accept us for who we are, even if they don't agree with all our actions. Confidentiality is part of trust. If a house church agrees that what is said in church will be held in confidence, much more sharing of ourselves is apt to take place. It also makes a difference *when* we choose to share our deeper selves. Griffin's point is that the appropriate moment in a relationship to disclose ourselves is when we feel that the other is willing to be self-disclosing as well. In relationships, there is always risk and that risk is a part of the life of Christian servanthood.

Church is more than just a weekly reminder of our commitment to the way of Christ. Church is a place for developing relationships and living out those relationships according to the way of Christ. The church is the model community, the city on the hill, that demonstrates what it is like when people live as Christ to each other. That community develops as we share ourselves with each other. It develops as we are in relationship with others who help us discover who it is that God wants us to be. Private meditation is part of our spiritual journey, but it is only as we are in relationship with others that we can discover the rest of who it is that God wants us to be.

Pastoral Care

Sometimes our needs for sharing can be met with the total house church. Other times it will be more helpful to talk with one other person about our concerns or problems or spiritual questions. To listen to someone in the name of Christ is to pastor him, to shepherd her. Each of our house churches has one or two persons designated as "shepherds," persons to whom anyone can come to find a caring listener, a gentle guide. People are free to choose anyone in the church to talk to about their problems. But it is helpful to designate shepherds so that people know there is always someone to whom they can go for help.

Shepherds are not professional counselors. When a problem seems too big for their skills, they should promptly help the person find someone with more training who can help. But most of us do not need professional counseling. We need someone who can listen to us and help us sort out the issues that are troubling us.

The Covenant Presbyterian Church in West Lafayette, Indiana, has offered the following suggestions for shepherds and other listeners on how to help people in times of trouble.

1. Relax. When someone is distressed, in trouble, or needing help, we immediately want to go to their rescue. Don't be a rescuer—relax. We think it is all up to us. We must solve everyone's problems. Problems are not solved that way. They are solved through a working process—often painful and necessarily that way. Pain is a crucial part of life; we grow through pain. It is not all up to you. Crisis and trouble will come in life, and we are equipped to handle what life brings. We have the capacity to endure just about anything. You know that from your experience. Relax. That communicates acceptance.

2. Listen. Forget you. Don't tell people all you know. When they are hurting, they don't hear you anyway. If you quote Scripture, you may only increase guilt. Crisis, pain, trouble, and conflict have to be expressed. Let the person tell it, as much as he or she chooses to tell. Create the atmosphere. If you are relaxed, he or she will tell you. (Caution: Let the person have the right not to tell you everything.) You can't stage confidence. It must be earned, and it takes time. They know you are a shepherd and that may in some people trigger a negative feeling. They might remember a person who was so helpful and turned out to be the gossip that told all the intimate secrets. It is shattering to be vulnerable and then have it backfire.

3. Honor the confidentiality of the person. Don't repeat anything. Assume it is confidential. If you think something should be repeated to another shepherd or anyone else, get permission. If the answer is no, honor that wish.

4. Reinforce. Reinforcement is full acceptance of the person. It communicates confidence, understanding, and trust. Reinforcement is affirmation. We can't reinforce too much because we all need it constantly.

5. Pray. In prayer we articulate our own feelings. We get them out to God. If we don't know what to do or say, we tell it to God. God works with our feelings and helps us to do the right thing. There is no substitute for the guidance of the Holy Spirit. The Holy Spirit is still the best Teacher. What I need to know or hear, more than anything else, is that someone is praying for *me*.

Sharing in Suffering

A lot of us spend our lives trying to avoid suffering. We run from conflict. We shrink from doing what is difficult, or procrastinate as long as possible. We try to stay away from people we are afraid will hurt us. We try to protect ourselves and make ourselves less vulnerable to suffering. But some suffering happens anyway. Sometimes people do hurt us. Our loved ones die or leave. We get sick. We feel lonely.

We overcome suffering by going through the center of the pain, rather than avoiding it. We risk the conflict, rather than avoiding talking to the person with whom we disagree. We feel our grief when we lose someone close to us. We uncover those hidden parts of ourselves that are contributing to our pain.

What enables us to move through this suffering and beyond it is people who care who are walking beside us. To walk beside and support those who are taking the risk of encountering their pain is the true task of shepherding. Shepherds allow those who suffer to express their pain and to find in that sharing of suffering a togetherness that gives them the strength to continue to move through that pain. Shepherds give us the encouragement we need to keep working at the arduous task of living a life of risk, of responding to oppression and violence done to us and others not with our own oppression and hate, but with love for the enemy and maintaining our own convictions and dignity.

Shepherds also serve as guides. Shepherds do not do the hard work of discovery for us. Instead, they help us discover the way of the Spirit for ourselves. Shepherds can steer troubled people around the pitfalls and discourage them from going down blind alleys. They can show us the maps that others have found useful in dangerous regions.

The meaning of suffering is one of the most difficult questions of human existence. We find that meaning as we stand with each other through times of suffering and seek to mold ourselves after the image of Jesus the Christ, who suffers with us and is risen to new life.

It is tempting to want to relate only to those who are not too different from ourselves. We may shrink from contact with those who are suffering from major illness or approaching death. We may find it hard to relate to the person who is poor or from a different ethnic background. We may have a difficult time listening with love to the long-winded person who is, on the surface, so convinced of his or her own superiority to the rest of the human race.

This is the point at which shepherds need to confront our own suffering, our own woundedness. To listen to the one who is suffering reminds me of my own suffering. To be with the victim brings back to me the times when I have been victimized in some way. Shepherds will not be able to communicate acceptance and real encouragement to those in pain until the shepherds themselves are willing to share their own pain and then move through it and beyond it to new life. To be a shepherd without burning out is to be in the process of healing those wounds of our own past which block our responses to the present.

For that to happen, shepherds also need to be shepherded. No one in the church need stand on a pedestal of righteous living which prohibits him or her from expressing pain and finding nurture. That is why the role of the shepherd should be shared. If a house church has only one shepherd, then there need to be open lines of communication with a shepherd in another house church.

We become family as we share our humanness and our pain with each other. We move toward loving each other unconditionally as we expose our wounds to each other and together offer them to God for healing. Then we can love people for themselves, not just our ideal of what they ought to be, or our hopes for them. We don't always choose our brothers and sisters in God's family, any more than we choose our biological brothers and sisters. This is the family God has given us. As we share our pain and our joy, we learn to love that family, and they love us.

Reflection and Action

1. Reflect on the words of Jesus in Mark 3:34-35: "Here are my mother and my brothers! Whoever does the will of God is my brother, and sister, and mother" (RSV).

2. What are you willing to share in the church? What would encourage you to share more? With what size group are you willing to share yourself? With a group of one hundred? A group of ten? Only one other person?

3. Where is the pain in your own life that needs healing? Can you share it with God? Can you share it with someone else in the church?

Chapter 7

Discipling

Our covenant as a church begins, "We commit ourselves to following Jesus Christ. . . ." The rest of the covenant spells out more about what that means. But our covenant is more than a set of rules which we commit ourselves to follow. We commit ourselves not primarily to the rules but to a person and to following his way. As members of the church we have chosen to model ourselves after the image of Christ.

Being a part of the covenant means more than just not breaking the rules: you shall not steal, or you shall not punch anyone in the nose, or you shall not be absent from church without a good reason. We can follow all the rules without following Christ.

Our ethic, instead, is a center-weighted ethic. Some of the edges may be defined less clearly than others. But the center—the way of Jesus—is clear, and we commit ourselves to moving toward that center. A center-weighted ethic does not abolish the rules; it goes beyond them toward positive action. This is what Jesus talked about in the Sermon on the Mount. He said, "Think not that I have come to abolish the law and the prophets; I have come not to abolish them but to fulfill them" (Matt. 5:17, RSV). Then he went beyond the law: not only "You shall not kill," but "First be reconciled with your brother and then come and offer your gift" at the altar. Not only "Love your neighbor," but "Love your enemies." Not only justice for the oppressors ("an eye for eye"), but treating them with kindness and generosity.

But how do we do that? What keeps us from drifting in some direction away from the center? Sometimes we are like the apostle Paul, who wrote, "I do not understand what I do; for I don't do what I would like to do, but instead I do what I hate" (Rom. 7:15, TEV). Or what keeps us as a church from drifting apart from each other, each doing his or her own thing, some uncomfortable with the behavior of others, but feeling powerless to do anything about it?

The answer is to help make each other better disciples of Christ. To make disciples is a process that begins with evangelism of nonbelievers and continues after baptism. This process has sometimes been called church discipline.

We may have a negative image of church discipline if we remember only the times when it was administered in a legalistic, punitive way—in some churches, only in the case of sexual sins. Or we may have no image of church discipline if we have come out of churches where it simply was not practiced, and every matter of Christian behavior was left to the individual. "The answer to bad church discipline is good church discipline, not no church discipline," wrote Marlin Jeschke in *Discipling the Brother: Congregational Discipline According to the Gospel.*[1]

House churches, because of their small size, have the opportunity to practice good church discipline, that is, discipling each other with love and accountability. Where people know each other well, where they have shared deeply with each other, where they care for each other, there people can hold each other accountable in the manner described in Galatians 6:1-2: "Brothers and sisters, if someone is overtaken in any trespass, you who are spiritual should restore that person in a spirit of gentleness. Look to yourselves, lest you, too, be tempted. Bear one another's burdens, and so fulfill the law of Christ" (author's translation).

Where the church is small enough for close relationships, people can disciple each other in ways which are not judgmental, but designed to help guide people in their own discovery of what it means to follow Jesus. The church can accept people's confessions of failure to do that, not with harsh criticism, but with guiding questions, "What is blocking you from doing what you would like to do?" or "Why do you think it is so hard to find time?" The emphasis is not just on following the rules, but on modeling our lives so that we, too, are "in Christ," incarnating Christ in the world today.

If Your Brother or Sister Sins Against You

If discipling in its broad sense is helping each other become more Christlike, one part of that broad task is confronting the brother or sister who has sinned against us. The key Scripture is Matthew 18:15-20:

> If your brother sins against you, go and tell him his fault, between you and him alone. If he listens to you, you have gained your brother. But if he does not listen, take one or two others along with you, that every word may be confirmed by the evidence of two or three witnesses. If he refuses to listen to them, tell it to the church; and if he refuses to listen even to the church, let him be to you as a Gentile and a tax collector. Truly, I say to you, whatever you bind on earth shall be bound in heaven, and whatever you loose on earth shall be loosed in heaven. Again I say to you, if two of you agree on earth about anything they ask, it will be done for them by my Father in heaven. For where two or three are gathered in my name, there am I in the midst of them. (RSV)

The primary purpose of confronting the erring brother or sister, in the passage, is to "gain the brother," that is, to restore the relationship. If someone has sinned against you, and you do not confront him or her, there is a barrier between you and that person. You no longer communicate freely. You may feel uncomfortable in that person's presence. So you go to the person you feel is at fault in order to clear up the matter. The purpose is not to punish the other person, but to mend a broken relationship.

You may find the other person feels you also were at fault. Perhaps mutual confession is needed. Or perhaps the brother or sister did not realize that he or she had offended you and is now willing to make amends. If so, the matter can stop here.

Many house churches and communities have discovered that following the procedure of Matthew 18 is a great gossip preventive. To go first to the person who I feel has done me wrong means that I do not talk about the problem first with my spouse or my friends whom I am trying to get on my side. The smaller the conflict, the more likely it can be managed. This process also means awareness that other people may be trying to "triangle" me, to bring me into the conflict before they have talked to the offending party. One person's response to such attempts is to ask, "And when are you planning to talk to her about this?"

Only if the difficulty cannot be managed at the one-to-one level is it wise to bring in one or two others—someone with more spiritual wisdom or experience, someone who can listen carefully to both sides, perhaps a shepherd, elder, or other church leader. If that still doesn't bring about an understanding or a change of behavior, only then does the matter go to the whole church.

This passage is one of only two in the Gospels which uses the Greek word for "church." In this passage, Jesus promises his presence where two or three are gathered in his name to decide in matters of binding (withholding fellowship) or loosing (forgiving)—or, as the terms are sometimes interpreted, forbidding or permitting. The gathered church has the authority to discipline those who persist in sinning, not for the purpose of punishment or of protecting the church's reputation, but to be able to continue calling people to model themselves after Christ with a clear conscience and without a sense of collective guilt for permitting the sin (the moving away from Christ) to continue.

The most loving act may be to call the erring person to accountability to the covenant he has made with Christ and the church, rather than to condone his disregard for the covenant. Even if the situation would go to the rare action of excluding a person from the fellowship, the intent is not to get rid of the problem, but to continue inviting the person back into the Christian community, to treat her "as a Gentile and a tax collector," still a person whom God loves and wants to become a child of God.

It is easier to conduct this process of confrontation, discernment, and restoration in a house church than in a large church where members may not always know each other.

John Howard Yoder has written:

> We understand more clearly and correctly the priority of the congregation when we study what it is that it is to do. It is only in the local face-to-face meeting, with brethren and sisters who know one another well, that this process can take place of which Jesus says that what it has decided stands decided in heaven. Whether the outcome be the separating of fellowship or its restoration, the process is not one which can be carried on in a limited time and by means of judicial formalities; it demands conversation of a serious and patient and loving character. Only when people live together in the same city, meet together often,

and know each other well, can this "bearing of one another's burdens" be carried out in a fully loving way.

The church is defined by this process, not by a legal organization nor by a purely spiritual criterion.[2]

This kind of discipling will not happen in large groups where people are free to remain distant from each other. The typical church with a large Sunday morning worship service and various committees with well-limited functions allows people to avoid the discipling process if they choose. There need to be some structures for accountability in groups of a manageable size, where people have committed themselves to participate in the discipling process—in a house church, or perhaps a group of only two.

Structures of Accountability

Discipling is more than confronting the person who does wrong. Discipling is also a process of helping each other become more and more molded into the image of Christ. It is a process of holding each other accountable for living into the covenant to which we have committed ourselves.

One structure for keeping us accountable for practicing the spiritual disciplines and walking in the way of Christ is faithful friendship. Pilgrims Mennonite Church, Akron, Pennsylvania, calls these faithful friends "accountability partners"—pairings that share personal and spiritual lives together. Louise Spiker has written in *No Instant Grapes in God's Vineyard,*

> While it is not impossible to keep Christian spiritual disciplines on our own, it is very difficult without someone to check regularly that we are actually doing what we have said we want to do. We are fallible beings. Paul knowingly speaks of the human condition when he says, "I do not understand what I do;

for I don't do what I would like to do, but instead I do what I hate" (Rom. 7:15). We need another person who cares enough to ask, "How are you?" and then listens with acceptance when we dare answer how it really is with us.[3]

Faithful friendship has a long history in the church. In monastic orders, monks and nuns had spiritual directors who could guide their journey toward God. Even if we do not have a spiritual director available with training in this area, we can still experience this support and guidance through faithful friendship—a kind of mutual spiritual direction between two persons. Teresa of Avila, a Spanish nun of the sixteenth century, wrote,

> Even though they be not in a religious Order, it would be a great thing for them to have someone to whom they could go, as many people do, so that they might not be following their own will in anything, for it is in this way that we usually do ourselves harm. They should not look for anyone (as the saying has it) cast in the same mould as themselves who always proceeds with great circumspection; they should select a man who is completely disillusioned with the things of the world. It is a great advantage for us to be able to consult someone who knows us, so that we may learn to know ourselves. And it is a great encouragement to see that things which we thought impossible are possible to others, and how easily these others do them. It makes us feel that we may emulate their flights and venture to fly ourselves, as the young birds do when their parents teach them.[4]

In a faithful friendship, the two persons agree to meet regularly with each other, usually every one or two weeks. They decide for what disciplines they wish to be held accountable. These disciplines could include daily meditation and prayer, Scripture study, journaling, recording dreams, diet, exercise, service to others, and additional reading that the faithful friends may wish to do together. At their regular meetings, faithful friends share a written accountability report with each other. Where during the last week or two weeks was I faithful and where did I fall short of my goals? What were the issues that surfaced during my journaling that I would like to share with my faithful friend? What were the highs and lows of my week? Then faithful friends can listen to each other.

Listen to each other with your inner ear, wrote Dorothy Devers, author of the book *Faithful Friendship*, as you communicate to one another how your reading and daily meditation and praying have changed your life—or perhaps have not. Be available to your faithful friend in every possible way. Seek to be helpful in concrete ways. Be understanding, but do not sidestep confrontation when confrontation is necessary. Always proceed with discretion and with love. Speak the truth in love as you are enabled to speak it from your own experience, humbly and honestly.[5]

One good way to begin is to share with your faithful friend your spiritual autobiography. This can recall the formative influences in your life, the forces, circumstances, persons, and events that have made you the person you are. Where in your life have you experienced repentance and change of heart? Where have you heard God calling you to new ventures? Then you and your faithful friend may wish to read together some of the many books now available on journaling, spirituality, meditation, dreams, faithful friendship, and spiritual direction.

The aim of faithful friendship is spiritual growth: growing both in our love for God and in our love for neighbor and growing in our ability to listen for God's call to serve in the world. As we grow in our ability to love and to listen to God, then we grow in Christlikeness. We are enabled to live out our covenant with Christ and the church in a fuller way.

Another structure of accountability is the annual sharing of one's spiritual pilgrimage in the house church. In Mennonite Church of the Servant, we do this annually, just before we covenant for the first time or recovenant with the church on Holy Thursday. During the three months before this time, house churches take some time to listen to the spiritual pilgrimage of everyone who wishes to covenant with the church. Sometimes one or two persons present a spiritual pilgrimage in an evening. Or a house church may choose to spend all day hearing everyone's pilgrimage. People covenanting for the first time may give a spiritual autobiography of what has led them from childhood to the place of covenanting with this church. Those who have already covenanted with the church may cover only the past year: how have they been faithful or unfaithful to the covenant?

Here are some guidelines for sharing spiritual pilgrimages:

1. Give a brief history of your spiritual development, your relationship with God, your relationship with the church.

2. During the past year, what have been your significant relationships in giving and receiving?

3. How have you related to others in the church?

4. How have you related to the unchurched, to people at work, to your family, and so forth?

5. What books and articles have you read? What classes have you taken?

6. What goals have you reached in Bible study, prayer, journaling, and other spiritual disciplines?

7. What is the state of your physical, spiritual, and psychological wellness?

8. How have you been a steward of time?

9. How have you been a steward of money and possessions?

10. How have you been involved in social and political concerns?

11. What are your goals for the next year? How do these in-

volve your house church and the church as a whole?

12. What are your life goals for five years from now? Ten years from now?

13. Can you affirm the covenant of this church as the direction for your life?

14. Do you wish to covenant with this house church and with the whole church for the coming year?

Our house churches have welcomed the process of giving spiritual pilgrimages as a more structured way to ask each other, "How has it been with you?" In fact, each year several people who are not ready to covenant with the church and are not required to give their spiritual pilgrimages choose to do so anyway. They like the structure for sharing something of themselves with the house church. Because they have shared more deeply they can feel more loved and affirmed for who they are and not just for the image they sometimes project.

Love and Accountability

To help each other follow Jesus Christ means both to love and to hold each other accountable. The greatest strength of the house church is the opportunity it gives us to be both known and loved for who we are. In the house church we recognize how difficult it is to try to be Christians on our own. We are not Lone Rangers. We need the help of other Christians as we seek to model ourselves after the suffering love of Jesus. We do not have to bear the cross alone. We can bear each other's burdens and help each other find the path toward God. We can encourage each other, support each other, confront each other. We can speak the truth to each other in love.

Both love and accountability are part of honest relationships. In those relationships we help each other follow Jesus Christ. And we build the ties of love among each other in the church.

Reflection and Action

1. In what conflict situations have you been recently which could have been managed more easily if you had followed Matthew 18 and gone first to the offending person?

2. For what spiritual disciplines and service in the world would you like to be held accountable? To whom do you want to be held accountable?

Chapter 8

Decisions

My first assumption about decision-making in the house church is that it is appropriate for the church to be making decisions. Somehow churches have to decide when to worship, where to meet, how to structure themselves, who is a member, how to include children in the church, and so forth.

My conviction is that making decisions together is not an unfortunate necessity, something we have to get out of the way so we can go on with the business of really being the church. Instead, making decisions is an essential part of being the church.

In the New Testament, the word usually translated "church" is *ekklesia*. This Greek word can mean any gathering of people, but it also has a narrower meaning: "a gathering of people in a town for political decision making." *Ekklesia* is the word used in the Greek version of the Old Testament to translate the assembly of God, the gathering of all Israel, or its representatives, for worship or decision-making.

In the Gospels, the word "church" is used only twice: in Matthew 16:18-19 in connection with the Great Confession and the church's power in binding and loosing, allowing and disallowing; and in Matthew 18:17 in connection with conflict resolution in the church.

In Acts and the Epistles, many of the references to church are general, or connected with worship and prayer. But many references are also related to decision-making. In Acts 13:1-3, the church at Antioch sets apart Barnabas and Saul for mission work. In Acts 15:22, the church agrees on representatives to report the decision on circumcision of Gentiles. First Corinthians 6:1-11 deals with the need for conflict resolution within the church rather than taking intrachurch disputes to the secular courts.

We can conclude that making decisions together was an integral part of being the church in the New Testament. We are the church just as much at our meetings for business as at our meetings for worship or study. Whether we are part of the larger gathered church or the smaller house church, we make decisions as the church.

Conflict

We all wish for the unity of the Holy Spirit in our decision-making. Keith Harder has written in the journal *Coming Together*,

> We have been profoundly touched by the prayer of Jesus in John 17 "that they all may be one," the description of the Jerusalem community in Acts 4 having "one heart and soul," the challenge of Paul in Philippians 2 to be "of the same mind, having the same love, being in full accord and of one mind," and the revelation in Ephesians 1:10 that it is the purpose of God in the fullness of time "to unite all things in heaven and things on earth." These and other Scriptures have burned their way into our hearts. Giving ourselves to God is to give ourselves to the unifying and reconciling purpose of God.[1]

Yet our idealism about unity in the church is soon shattered by the real-life conflicts that we encounter there. We find that conflict is inevitable. In fact, in the house church, conflicts seem to increase, and some may begin to long for the impersonal atmosphere of the large church where people kept their distance and avoided conflict.

The closer the relationship, the more intense the conflict. The closer the relationship, the more frequent the conflict. We cannot have it any other way. We come to unity and intimacy, not by working around the conflict, but by going through its center, by accepting both the uncertainties of conflict and its benefits.

Conflict, in itself, is not bad. Conflict is a sign that we are involved with each other, that we have taken the time to know each other with all our differences. In conflict, we are able to recognize our differences and affirm our individual uniqueness. To affirm conflict means that we have taken time to listen to the differences that each has expressed. Conflict also means that we care about continuing the relationship. If the relationship with you meant nothing to me, I would just walk away and not bother with the pain of conflict. I avoid conflict with the anonymous driver who pulled out in front of me because we may never meet again. If I value my relationship with you, I will work through our conflict so that we can continue to be friends and not have a list of controversial topics that we cannot talk about with each other. To face our conflict means that I want to have a transparent relationship with you in which we can relax and be open with each other.

Because we have come through the conflict together we are closer to each other. We have a stronger relationship than we did at the beginning. We know that our caring for each other is not dependent on always expressing agreement with each other. We can disagree and still be friends.

Conflict also helps the church clarify its goals and ideas. Before our congregation was faced with the conflict over whether to accept the gift of a building, we had not talked much about the issue of church growth. How big did we want to get as a total church? What did we want to do to incorporate new people into the church? The conflict helped us identify an important issue for the future.

Conflict also helps groups define themselves. Who are we? What is acceptable behavior here? What is in and what is out? Conflict helps individuals define their identity, too. As we engage in conflict, I understand better who you are and I discover more about myself and what I am willing to stand up for or give in on.

Finally, through conflict, new and creative solutions may emerge. Conflict disturbs the status quo. It creates the conditions for change, change which can be beneficial to the group. Through the discussion, new ideas may come forth offering a better way of doing things than either party to the conflict had considered previously.

Conflict can be beneficial to a house church. But we all know of conflicts that were not beneficial, that were damaging to relationships and self-esteem. There are times when we all need some fair-fight training.

Fighting fair means no name calling; talk about the issues instead. It means being authentically involved in the conversation rather than disengaged, seeming to have one's mind somewhere else. It means talking about specifics, not vague generalities: "I think . . ." not "some people think. . . ." Fighting fair means using humor appropriately, rather than for sarcasm or ridicule. It means giving accurate feedback to the other party: "I hear you saying . . ." and then waiting until the other person says, "Yes, that is what I was saying." Fighting fair means talking about the here-and-now issue, not a list of grievances from the distant past. Fighting fair means listening to the person with an attitude of openness, ready to admit if I have been wrong or if someone else has a better idea than mine. Fighting fair also means being willing to state my position assertively, even if others do not agree, rather than quickly backing down and still being resentful.

Conflict within the church can be managed more readily if people are willing to experience confusion for a while, rather than quickly forming two sides with clear positions. Before people have dug in at their positions, it may be most helpful to talk about the confusion people are feeling. Brainstorm many alternate solutions. What are the goals we have in common but are not sure how to reach? Three or four or twenty possible solutions may emerge, some of them better than the two positions on which the church was tempted to polarize.

David Augsburger has suggested the following steps at restoring concord if the church has already polarized over an issue:

1. Accept the faith of the other. Trust in the Holy Spirit at work in the community implies accepting that everyone in dialogue is a person of faith as well as a person whose perspective and obedience is personal and partial.

2. Define the conflict: narrowly (focus on the smallest issue possible), neutrally (in simple, clear, single-level words that are inoffensive), mutually (in two-way, two-party language that includes both).

3. Clarify the issues by sharpening the contrasts. Avoid glossing over the differences. Instead, lift the central concerns to greater clarity. This invites others to identify with or disassociate themselves from the various sides.

4. Reflect. Encourage critical self-analysis. Invite each to examine personal needs invested in the outcome and to assess whether the ends desired are worth the cost of obtaining them.

5. Replay. Require each side to replay the other side's position in a way acceptable to the other side. Although repetitious,

the reporting process pays off in trust of the other's perceptions.

6. Choose a joint goal or goals. Find options which offer mutual gain. Try to find joint solutions satisfactory to both.

7. Celebrate the larger, deeper convictions on which both sides agree. Reaffirm that the issues debated and resolved are secondary to the primary convictions that unite us.[2]

Consensus

A method for decision-making that seeks to find joint goals, or a solution in which all sides can win, is consensus. Many ways of making decisions as a group tend to come up with win-lose solutions. A majority imposes its solution on the minority. Victory may bring feelings of elation to the winners, but defeat brings feelings of rejection, failure, and impotence to the losers. The losing party, while forced to accept a solution, will often continue the conflict either openly or behind others' backs and sooner or later try to get a more favorable outcome. Win-lose methods like majority-rule voting may reach decisions quickly, but decisions may be implemented slowly, or they may need to be redecided as the disgruntled minority still seeks to find a satisfactory solution.

Consensus, on the other hand, is a win-win solution. Its central concern is that each view or idea be heard and understood before it is tested. Consensus seeks to allow time for the church to discuss all the considerations thoroughly. It seeks to involve all members in the process of making the decision. It seeks to find those solutions with which no one disagrees.

Consensus may take much longer than Robert's Rules of Order as a process for decision-making. But the decisions thus made are more apt to stick and be carried out with enthusiasm by more people in the church. Douglas Steere has written concerning the use of consensus among the Quakers, for whom the process has had a long tradition:

The Quaker business meeting is not a process that will commend itself to the driven ones who demand a swift decision. There is a Finnish proverb that says, "The God of Finland is never in a hurry." Neither are Friends who have been seasoned in this approach to reaching decisions. There is a story of a man who had been conducting a study of the longevity of members of different religious denominations. He told his friend about visiting a Quaker cemetery and of having been appalled at finding by the birth and death dates on the small headstones that these Quakers seemed to live longer than those of any other denomination he had come upon. His friend replied that he should not have been surprised at that if he knew anything about Quakers, for it always took them longer than anyone else to make up their minds about anything![3]

At The Assembly, Goshen, Indiana, consensus is practiced at the congregational members' meetings. First, the congregational elders propose and announce the agenda for a meeting. They are to test each item for adequate preparation before including it on the proposed agenda.

Before discussion of an item, someone other than the moderator of the meeting should present basic information or summarize previous information and work.

If two or more points of view emerge, the moderator should try to have each view presented separately, with initial testing only for understanding. Discussion then follows.

If new considerations emerge or many questions and feelings are present, the meeting may break into small groups to assess where people are, project work needed, and suggest next steps.

The moderator should occasionally summarize, keeping the discussion focused on the task to be done. From time to time the moderator may ask, "Is this what we are saying?"

The moderator should encourage all members of the group to participate in the discussion.

The moderator tests for consensus and then declares it when the process reaches that stage of agreement. A consensus may not represent complete agreement in all instances. But where some differences remain, it represents the willingness of a minority to allow the discussion to be concluded and to join with the decision of the group, perhaps with a heavy heart, in recognition of the leading of many brothers and sisters and the sense of the group as a whole.

Consensus does not mean that every member of the meeting feels equally happy about the decision reached. Steere has noted,

> The kind of unanimity that is referred to is a realization on my part that the matter has been carefully and patiently considered. I have had a chance at different stages of the process ... to make my point of view known to the group, to have it seriously considered and weighed. Even if the decision finally goes against what I initially proposed, I know that my contribution has helped to sift the issue, perhaps to temper it, and I may well have, as the matter has patiently taken its course, come to see it somewhat differently from the point at which I began. I might go so far as to agree with a French writer, deVigny, who said, "I am not always of my own opinion." I have also come to realize that the group as a whole finds the resolution that seems best to them. When this point comes, if I am a seasoned Friend, I no longer oppose it. I give it my *Nihil Obstat* [nothing is objectionable], and I emerge from the meeting not as a member of a bitter minority who feels outflanked and rejected, but rather as one who has been through the process of the decision and is willing to abide by it even though my own accent would not have put it in this form.

Without this kind of participative humility, the Quaker business meeting process is seriously hampered. I have seen a clerk in my own meeting tenderly defer to one member who felt strongly opposed to an action that the group was ready to accept, and after a matter of a few months' time this person was no longer unwilling for it to proceed.[4]

The Role of the Dissenter

The closer the members of the house church, the more threatening it seems when one member dissents. Groups put a lot of pressure on deviant members to conform to the group norms. The dissenter seems to threaten the unity of the group.

But there is some evidence that deviancy is not a personality trait. Deviancy is a label conferred by the group upon those who act differently in some way, according to Em Griffin, author of *Getting Together: A Guide for Good Groups*.[5] Groups have a way of creating the role of the dissenter.

That is not all bad, Griffin has written. A little bit of deviance helps a group get where it wants to go! Without any deviance, a group will flounder. Everyone will be nicey-nice. No one will be quite sure what is acceptable behavior and what is out-of-bounds. More than that, groups without dissenters will have little creativity. Creativity is, by definition, deviance. From dissenters come new, creative, more efficient ways of doing things. As long as the dissenter is not calling into question the core values of the house church, the dissenting can be healthy and the church will be stronger for it.

But two or more chronic dissenters in a small group of eight, for example, are probably more than the group can handle, especially if each is pulling in opposite directions. In congregations with more than one house church, it might be easier to suggest that one of them join a different house church—or increase the size of their house church to ten or twelve so that it is large enough to absorb more dissenters. But most of the time, the best way to deal with dissenting is simply to enjoy it and listen to those with dissenting views. All of us have only partial truth revealed to us, and the dissenter may have partial truth that complements what we know.

In working by consensus, the chronic dissenter poses a special problem, if we think that consensus means that everyone must agree. Some dissenters seem never to agree with the group on the subject! The Fellowship of Hope, Elkhart, Indiana, has suggested the following guidelines for consensus amid diversity:

1. Each individual is called to set aside his or her own will in order to know the will of the Lord.

2. The Lord can speak through any member of the body.

3. Decisions of the body never reflect the full wisdom of God, so we need to be respectful of one another's differing insights into God's truth, even when we choose a certain direction over others. Past decisions can be reviewed and changed when deeper wisdom is revealed.

4. When an individual or small number of persons differs from the rest of the body, they sometimes bear the deeper wisdom of God; sometimes they do not. The careful and sensitive testing of minority opinions is a necessary part of the decision-making process. Such testing sometimes results in the emergence of new perspectives and solutions; sometimes the result is to ask persons to subordinate their concerns to the rest of the body.[6]

In some cases, the moderator will ask the chronic objector if his or her dissenting opinions can be recorded in the minutes and then set aside so the that the body can move ahead. In other cases, the church may choose to wait and continue the decision-making process at another time, when there may be more agreement.

In my experience in house churches, the greater problem is not that someone is always choosing to dissent, but that the group often is forcing a person into that role. I have observed that when a new issue is discussed, someone in the church will suggest to the person who has been labeled as the "dissenter" that he or she will undoubtedly dissent on this issue, too. It takes assertiveness on the part of the "dissenter" to tell the group, "No, I am not dissenting on this issue." It takes an attitude of openness and listening on the part of the rest of the group to allow people to change their minds and not to point out publicly how this new viewpoint is not consistent with their viewpoint last month.

The Unity of the Spirit

No matter how much we say about the right methods of decision-making, unity in decisions is still a gift from God's Spirit. Learning good methods of relating to each other in decision-making is important. I do not want to minimize the importance of using our intellect and our analytical skills as best we can. On critical issues we need to use all our skills and bring all the parts of ourselves to the issue. If we refuse to bring our whole selves to the decision, we will arrive at only partial truth. But that is not enough.

We need also to seek the will of God and the power of God's Spirit to bring unity to a divided church. I have repeatedly seen the Spirit of God bring about consensus where it seemed that none was possible.

To be in touch with the Spirit it is good to conduct each meeting for decision-making in a spirit of prayer, just as much so as if it were a meeting for worship. In Mennonite Church of the Servant we recently experienced the power of prayer in decision-making in an exciting way. We had been offered the free gift of a building by a company for which one of our members worked. Some people in the church leaned toward accepting the building. Others leaned toward not taking the building. Most were not certain what was the right decision. We spent one evening discussing the issue, but without gaining much clarity on what we should do.

We did decide to meet two days later, not for discussion, but for prayer. After some initial sharing of new information, we spent twenty minutes in silence and listening prayer together. Then we went around the circle saying what we had learned in the silence.

We discovered we had consensus on part of the decision: that we would not buy adjacent land. But more than that, many people in the circle reported that they felt a new sense of unity in the church, a willingness to work on new goals, and a need to decide on the future shape of our church.

At the next meeting, a month later, we again spent twenty minutes in silent prayer and then went around the circle again. We now had consensus. All either wanted to take the building, or they did not wish to stand in the way of that decision. What had seemed like an impossible decision had become possible by listening to the Spirit through prayer.

This kind of decision-making means giving up one's personal need to be right or to have one's own way and, instead, seeking God's way. It means recognizing the partiality of my opinions. It means waiting on God—sometimes for what seems a long time.

In my case, it meant searching myself for feelings that were blocking my hearing God's Spirit on this matter. It meant freeing myself from old bondages and being willing to set aside past loyalties. Then I could really listen to the Spirit.

We decided to depend on the Holy Spirit to lead us into unity. What was impossible for us human beings was possible with God. The truth which we discovered that evening is still partial truth. In these days we still see through a glass dimly. But by listening for the message of the Spirit we saw more clearly. Our unity was truly a gift of the Spirit.

Reflection and Action

1. What is your style of conflict? Do you usually give in? Do you need to win at all costs? Do you avoid conflict by leaving the situation? Do you seek a compromise? Do you try to find a mutually satisfactory solution? What style of conflict do you want to use most of the time? How can you move toward this goal? What barriers or fears are preventing you from approaching conflict in the way you would like?

2. Think of an issue on which your house church or other small group had varying opinions. If the church reached consensus, how did that happen? If the church did not use the method of consensus, imagine how using consensus might have changed the outcome.

3. Can you identify a dissenter in your house church? In what instances have you felt the group pushing that person into a dissenting role? Why does the group need that role? Do others in the church sometimes play the role of the dissenter, or is that the responsibility of just one person?

Chapter 9

Gifts

In the church, we all are gifted. That is the assumption with which I have begun, and I have never yet found anyone in the church who did not have a skill or ability or sensitivity which could not be valuable to the church in some way. I have found that my experience matches that described in 1 Corinthians 12, where Paul writes, "To *each* is given the manifestation of the Spirit for the common good" (v. 7, RSV, emphasis mine).

The house church is a good place to discover and use the gifts of the Spirit for two reasons. The house church is a small enough group of people to take time to help each other discover their gifts. Second, the smallness of the group makes it obvious that everyone's gifts are needed in order for the house church to function. The size of the church itself says, "We need you."

Steve Reschly of Cedar Community Mennonite Church has written:

> We have developed a strong sense of the universality of giftedness in the fellowship. There is no member who is not gifted for ministry. Every believer receives an ability (or abilities) indispensable to the congregation in its growth and love. Each gift is uniquely valuable in its own place and none can replace any other.[1]

Discovering Gifts

The first step in discovering one's gifts is often taken alone. In Mennonite Church of the Servant, we suggest that, before people come to their house church for gift discernment, they spend some time alone—thinking, praying, journaling. From Palmer Becker's *You and Your Options*,[2] we have adapted a series of questions for people to consider in discovering their gifts.

1. What do you like to do? List ten things that you enjoy doing? Then make notes beside each item indicating how that interest might be used in or through the church to build Christ's kingdom.

2. What are you able to do? Don't worry about whether you appear to be bragging. Experience the joy of affirming the good which has happened and is happening through you! Divide your life from age six until the present in six periods of time that are natural for you. Then list specific accomplishments for each period. Be so specific that you can name the time and place where they happened. Go over the lists of accomplishments and check the eight happenings which now seem the most significant. What skills did you use in these accomplishments?

3. What are your resources in time? health? education? experience? finances?

4. Look over the lists of gifts of the Spirit in Romans 12, 1 Corinthians 12, and Ephesians 4. In which of these areas are you strongest?

5. What values are most important to you? Property and financial security? Knowledge and truth? Peace and justice? Popularity and recognition? Beauty and pleasure? Harmony and family?

6. What are your goals: in education or experience, in relationships, in vocation and service, in spiritual development?

7. Now list four options for how you would like to use your gifts in the church. Which option would best use your top interest? Which option would best use your abilities? Which option would best use your strongest spiritual gift? To which option would you be willing to give the most time and energy? Which option would best respond to the most urgent needs in the world? Which option would help you most toward your most important goal? Which option would most help you to make disciples for Jesus Christ? Then write down, "My strongest calling at this time is to. . . ."

After this private discovery and testing, people take the gifts they are proposing to use to their house church for testing. Then with the house church each person decides on at least one gift for use in the church and plans next steps on how he or she will use that gift.

This process is not short. Our church suggests forty-five minutes per person in the house church as a minimum time for looking at a person's gifts and affirming what that person has suggested or suggesting other directions for use of his or her gifts. Some house churches stretch out this process over two months. Others have gone on a daylong retreat to discern gifts for the whole house church.

Neither is the process the same for each person. Some people may already be using gifts that have been affirmed by the church, and the current task may be to reaffirm those gifts. Others may not have come up with a gift to use in the church even after their private search through prayer and reflection. For these latter persons, the task of the house church is to encourage, to draw out of these persons the beauty that is already there, the unrecognized abilities waiting to be used. In our house church, one person came to the gift discernment meeting saying, "This is going to be short, because I don't have much to say." Before the meeting was over, we—and he—had discerned in him a gift of organizing: organizing the church bulletin board and library and starting a worship resource file.

It is also possible that the gift discerned for a person last year may be different from the gift discerned for her this year. New options may have emerged, or new abilities or self-confidence. Or new needs of the church may have emerged for which this person has the needed skills.

Using Gifts

Discerning gifts is good, but may be of no value until we can free people to use the gifts that have been discerned. Many of us need more than encouragement to use our gifts. Pulling the other or pushing ourselves to use our gifts may do little good if we do not remove the barriers that are hindering us and others from using our gifts.

Elizabeth O'Connor in *Eighth Day of Creation* has noted three barriers that keep us from using our gifts: jealousy, fear of failure, and lack of accountability. She has written, "A primary purpose of the church is to help us discover our gifts and, in the face of our fears, to hold us accountable for them so that we can enter into the joy of creating."[3]

We can help ourselves use our gifts if we deal, first of all, with feelings of jealousy. First Corinthians 12:14-26 speaks of the discord in the body when the foot wishes it were a hand, or the eye says it doesn't need the hand. Our jealous feelings are not helped by the connotation which the word "gifted" has acquired in our language. The gifted people are special people, we feel; there are not very many of them. They are the people of the 99th percentile. They are gifted; we are not.

That is not the language of the New Testament. First Corinthians 12 says that every member of the church has a gift. Possession of a gift is not dependent on intelligence, age, or spiritual maturity. If we take that seriously, it means there is something for every person in the church to do.

So we do not need to be jealous about someone else's gifts; we have gifts, too. We allow others to be different from us. We accept that their gifts may be different from ours. We celebrate the gifts that we do have, rather than worrying about our not having the same gifts that others have.

Fear of others' jealousy can also inhibit the use of gifts. We sometimes hesitate to use gifts we know we have because we fear the dislike of others. We are afraid that if we use our gifts, we will become to "set apart," too different. Here, too, we can remove this barrier if we accept and celebrate the fact that we are different: we are not all hands or all feet. The body of Christ functions better if the variety of gifts is present. The person jealous of my gift also has a gift. Perhaps my task is to help that person discover his gift so that he no longer needs to feel jealous. If I can affirm the gift of the other, I have no need to hide my gift.

The second barrier to exercising gifts in the church is fear of failure. It is natural to want not to fail. We want to appear capable to the people around us, and deep down there is the nagging notion that if we are not capable, we will not be lovable either. If we sing the wrong note in public, or make the wrong decision in a leadership position, or forget what we were supposed to do, or our project does not have the effect we wanted it to have, we are afraid that neither others nor ourselves—or maybe even God—will think we are worth loving. So we volunteer for nothing. Fear of failure immobilizes us by telling us that our worth as persons is dependent on our performance.

One remedy for fear of failure is to allow ourselves and others room to fail. If we hold each other accountable for the right use of our gifts, the purpose is not so that we can say to someone who fails, "You are not a good person because you failed." The purpose is to encourage the person to try again or to try something different while still affirming the worth of that person, which does not change with success or failure. We want to know that others in the church love us and God loves us, in spite of our success or failure.

We sometimes have the notion that all those inside the church are, or should be, sinless, perfect people. The view from the New Testament is not that those in the church have never failed, but that those in the church have been forgiven and have set out again on the right path. To join the church is to join the band of forgiven people—pilgrims together toward the glory of Christ—who are not afraid to risk because they can risk again. Failure is painful. But the pain is bearable and we can learn through the pain, if there are people around us who continue to love us and help us grow stronger because of the pain.

This means that we can claim the freedom to allow ourselves and others the opportunities to try out gifts we have only started to develop, because we know that if we fail we have a loving community that will give us room to explore and to grow toward the light of Christ.

Another barrier to our using our gifts is lack of accountability. We may identify gifts in a person, but then never check to see whether she is using that gift or whether he is doing what he said he would. Or we do not set a deadline by which a certain task should be done. In Mennonite Church of the Servant, this surfaced in the early years of the church's life with the choosing of shepherds, one or two persons within each house church who were to take primary responsibility for pastoral care. The house churches chose these people with some care and defined their duties. But because pastoral care was not usually a public matter, no one knew exactly what the shepherds were doing. The shepherds didn't even know what each other was doing. The situation improved when the shepherds began meeting regularly to discuss with each other what had been happening in their roles and in the congregation.

All of us are needed for the functioning of the body of Christ. When we overcome our fears and discover our special and particular gifts, using those gifts will bring forth a sense of excitement that we are sharing in the work of the church; we are needed.

The Gift of Visioning

Most churches—most groups of any kind—begin with a vision. One leader may be clearer about the vision of what the group is and wants to become, but the church really begins with a number of people who share a vision. In time, the church may find it hard to maintain its original vision. The person who articulated the first vision may have moved away. Other members may like the vision in theory, but have little commitment to making it happen. Without a structure for maintaining the vision, the vision can die and the church stagnates or dies.

The problem of maintaining a vision is more difficult for house churches than for "sanctuary-model" churches. The vision for a house church is not one with which most of us have grown up. More traditional churches often have an easier consensus on the shape of their congregations—what they all knew when they were children, the way it always has been, or what the denomination suggests to them that the church should be.

How can a vision survive and grow in a house church?

Visioning happens in worship, where we remind ourselves of our center in Christ. Those who lead worship have a responsi-

bility to structure the service in a way which builds and rein-
forces the church's vision. Visioning is sustained through a
church's written covenant. Vision happens through teaching
and learning. Classes are especially important to articulate the
vision to newcomers to the church. Shepherds, pastors, or
others involved in counseling and discipling can help individuals direct their lives according to that vision.

There is also need for visioning on behalf of the whole
church. Small-group research has shown that the most success-
ful groups are those with leaders who not only take the ideas of
other group members into consideration, but who provide the
group with vision and structure.

The primary functions of the visioner are to articulate the vision, work out its theology, warn the congregation when it is
departing from the vision, and adapt the vision to the new
situation. The role of the visioner is not necessarily connected
with administration, teaching, or shepherding. It is not the role
of an authoritarian leader. The visioner is the person other
church members have chosen to help them follow the direction
in which they said they wanted to be led when they
covenanted with the church.

Proverbs 29:18 says, "Where there is no vision, the people
perish" (KJV), or more literally, "Where there is no visioner,
the people go every which way." The gift of visioning keeps
house churches on the straight path.

The danger which visioners face is that they will love the vision more than the real people in their church. But that is when
the vision become death-giving rather than life-giving. That is
why visioning is not the only gift the church needs. The church
also needs those who shepherd others and listen to them.

The Gift of Shepherding
The metaphor of the shepherd is used in the Old Testament

for the king, who was to look after his people, to read and obey the law, and to encourage the people in obeying the law. In the New Testament, the metaphor of the shepherd is used of Jesus (see especially John 10), but also of those who are to lead the church. In John 21:15-19, Jesus commissioned Peter to "Feed my sheep." In Acts 20:25-31, Paul asked the elders of the church at Ephesus to "be shepherds of the church of God," keeping watch against distortion of the truth. In Ephesians 4:11, pastors—or shepherds—are mentioned together with teachers in the list of offices in the church. In 1 Peter 5:1-4, church elders are asked to be shepherds of God's flock that is under their care, being willing, eager to serve, and "not lording it over those entrusted to you, but being examples to the flock." The variety of terms in the New Testament for this role has given rise to the variety of titles which churches use for people in this role: shepherds, elders, pastors.

In the Mennonite Church of the Servant each house church has one or two shepherds. Their first responsibility is the spiritual oversight of their house church. The person with the gift of visioning may create and articulate the vision; the shepherd puts flesh on the vision and helps the church live out the vision.

Shepherds pay attention to both individual and churchwide concerns. Shepherds discuss the overall needs of the church. What need can the theme of the fall retreat address? Is our worship balanced in its approach? Should we start another house church? Are we as a church being faithful to the covenant to which we have committed ourselves? Shepherds also care about individual needs. Has Don found a house church to which he can belong? Does Maria need a listening ear?

We have adapted for our own shepherds' handbook the instructions to shepherds of Ernest Martin of the Midway Mennonite Church, Columbiana, Ohio.

Shepherding means:

1. Caring for people by showing interest and concern for them in the full range of life experience.

2. Giving encouragement and affirmation. We are the most effective in helping people when we are positive, affirming them, encouraging them, believing for change where change is needed.

3. Showing compassion and offering help. Some people have close friends to whom they turn in times of special need, but many do not.

4. Facilitating an exchange of resources within the congregation. You don't need to and shouldn't try to do everything for everybody. There are a lot of untapped energies and resources in the congregation which you can help release.

5. Being available even when there doesn't seem to be an opening for you to take initiative in any direct ministry.

In terms of specific actions, shepherding may mean listening to persons with problems. It may mean referring people to appropriate counseling beyond your capabilities. It means praying regularly for each person in your house church. It means visiting people individually, not just at house church meetings. It means being especially available at times of personal or family stress, including illness. It means helping new people become a part of the house church.

Shepherding is the work of pastoral care. People do not have to be trained in seminaries or graduate schools of psychology in order to practice Christian shepherding. Shepherding is caring—about people as individuals and about the church as a whole. It can be helpful, however, to develop training sessions for shepherds within the congregation so that they can feel more self-confident in their role and begin to use new skills. This last spring we engaged a nearby Christian mental health center to teach a series of classes on shepherding and listening skills. The Stephen Series is an interdenominational program to teach shepherding skills to lay people. Or a seminary-trained pastor could teach a class on pastoral care. Sensitive and caring Christians can learn to be shepherds and grow in the Christian way as they help others to grow.

The Gift of Listening

Closely related to the gift of shepherding is the gift of listening. There are people who may not be ready to be shepherds who nevertheless have the gift of listening. They are the people whom, although they may not be in an official leadership role, others seek out when they need someone to listen to them.

We often underestimate the value of just listening. People with problems do not usually want our advice. They certainly do not want our commands about what we should do next. They do need us to listen. They need us to play back to them what we are hearing. They need to talk to someone so that they themselves can hear and decide whether what they are thinking makes sense.

When people who come to us are under stress, we want to be the rescuer. We want to give help. We want to give the advice that will make them say, "Thanks! That's just what I'll do." But problems don't get solved by our doing it for them. Part of living is going through the pain of working through our own problems, coming to our own solutions, that we can claim and feel right about. The role of the listener is to assure people under stress that they are not alone and that they are loved.

In some cases, people who come to us may ask us for information that we have. But even if we have no advice nor information to dispense, we have still helped if we have simply listened and enabled them to recognize the presence of God in the midst of their pain.

The Gift of Community Building

Others among us have the gift of building community. They are the ones who organize celebrations. They recognize that part of being the church together is having good times together. They call us to remember that the basis of our life together is relationships. We build relationships not only in formal settings, but in informal conversations and doing things together.

In the Mennonite Church of the Servant, about half the members are intentional neighbors, that is, we live within a mile of each other—some of us next door to each other. Because we live closer, we can see each other more often, drop in at each other's houses with less excuse, and build relationships outside of regularly scheduled meetings. There are two or three people within the whole church who make it a point to invite people to live in the neighborhood, who hunt apartments for rent for others. They have the gift of building community.

Another member plans campouts, canoe trips, and other activities where people can spend more extended time together. He has the gift of building community.

Another way to build community is to invite new people into the church. Ideally, all of us do some of that, but some people have a stronger gift of evangelism. They radiate enthusiasm about the congregation and bring others to church to share the good news of what God is doing in the congregation.

Others are welcomers. Once new people are in church, they introduce themselves and welcome the newcomers. They make them feel at home and wanted. They also have the gift of building community.

Without the gift of community building, a church becomes stagnant or ingrown. The community builders communicate, "You are a part of us." That is the first word newcomers are waiting to hear.

The Gift of Administration

In order to function well, the church also needs people with the gift of administration. They are the organizers. They remember what it was we said we would do in July. They remind us to plan. Without them the church would function haphazardly.

In the Mennonite Church of the Servant, shepherds have part of the administrative role. They coordinate activities between house churches. They make sure that someone is taking charge of finding teachers for Christian education and planning worships. They do the first processing of decisions for the whole church and then make recommendations to the church life meeting. They make sure that someone is taking care of the church finances.

Beyond that, the church needs people with the gift of leading meetings. Good moderators of decision-making meetings are people who can set a clear agenda and keep a meeting moving on the subject, while still being sensitive to the movement of the Spirit in the meeting. It is helpful to have a designated leader say, "Now it is time to start," and "Now it is time to move on to something else." Leaderless groups of more than two or three people find it difficult to accomplish much— or else drag meetings on for hours. A good moderator is also sensitive to what people in the group are saying and is able to put together a statement to test for consensus.

There are also people with the gift of administration who do not have the up-front roles. They work quietly, sometimes unnoticed in organizing files, writing letters, typing newsletters, and straightening up. They also have a needed gift.

The Gift of Praying

Prayer is also a spiritual gift, manifested more in some than in others. While we all are to pray, privately and as a church, people with the gift of praying seem to be more sensitive to the times when we need to pray. They are the ones who stop us in the middle of a tense decision-making meeting with the request that we take ten minutes for silent prayer and asking for the guidance of the Spirit before we continue with dis-cussion. They are the ones with confidence that prayer will make a difference.

I have grown to value those among us who help us not only to learn about God, but to experience God. They help those bound up in a scientific-method worldview to recognize the reality of the spiritual world. They open others to the experience of meditation, visions, dreams, tongues, healing, and the other ways in which God touches us directly.

There is a gentleness about those with the gift of praying. They do not use prayer as a way to preach us a sermon. They find prayer a way of opening themselves and others to the power of God at work in the world.

The Gift of Teaching and Prophecy

I have combined my discussion of the gifts of teaching and prophecy because they have in common bringing us back to our center in Christ. The teacher connects the present with that center as found in the past, especially in Scripture. The prophet connects the present with the center as found in the future.

The teacher calls us to remember what God has done in the past and then helps us discern the meaning of that for the present. The prophet looks at the line of God's action and extends that line into the future. The prophet says, "If God keeps on acting in this way, this is what will happen," or "If God's principles are taken to their natural conclusion, this is what we should be doing in the new situation."

We need teachers and prophets with sound training, and we need to give them permission to exercise those gifts.

The Gift of Generosity

Those with the gift of generosity give of themselves and their possessions freely. They loan their lawn mowers and cars. They invite people to dinner. They have time to talk to us. They try not to accumulate too many things, lest they become too anxious about them. They help people paint their house. They offer to baby-sit. They offer guests a place to sleep. They remind us that what we have is ours in trust to use for building the community of God.

The Fullness of Christ

This listing of gifts is not meant to be complete. It is meant to illustrate the variety of gifts that are present in the church and that the church needs in order to function. I doubt, too, whether the apostle Paul's lists of gifts in 1 Corinthians 12, Ephesians 4, and Romans 12 were meant to be exhaustive. None of them are quite the same. Paul's point seems to be that the church needs a diversity of gifts in order to be the body of Christ. John Howard Yoder has written that the "fullness of Christ" in Ephesians 4:13 refers not to the Christian individual, but to the divinely coordinated multiple ministry. That is, we attain the fullness of Christ when we have many gifts for ministry at work in the church.[4] That is how we find the unity of the faith, knowledge of the Son of God, and mature adulthood. That is how, "speaking the truth in love, we grow up in every way into him who is the head, into Christ, from whom the whole body, joined and knit together by every joint with which it is supplied, when each part is working properly, makes bodily growth and upbuilds itself in love" (RSV).

The church is not an organization of active clergy and passive laity. The church is a community of active ministers, all called to ministry by our baptism, in which each may exercise a different ministry to build up the body of Christ. So the house church asks for a ministry for everyone. Dietrich Bonhoeffer has written:

> A community which allows unemployed members to exist within it will perish because of them. It will be well therefore if every member receives a definite task to perform for the community, that he may know in hours of doubt that he, too, is not useless and unusable.[5]

When we have identified a ministry for each member of the church, then we celebrate. It is not enough to discern gifts; we need to bring them into the open, tell people what they are, and celebrate them! Only then can we use them freely in the congregation. This last year when the house churches finished the gift discernment process for each person, we celebrated them as a whole church. Someone had made a poster in the shape of a building and each person was given a stone or brick made of paper on which to write his or her gift and name. Then all attached their "living stones" to the wall of the house of the Holy Spirit.

Reflection and Action

1. Study the calls of God to the heroes and heroines of the Bible to use their gifts: Moses (Exod. 3:1—4:20), Deborah and Barak (Judg. 4:1-10), Isaiah (Isa. 6:1-8), the suffering servant (Isa. 49:1-7), Jeremiah (Jer. 1:1-10), Samuel (1 Sam. 3:1-21), Ananias (Acts 9:1-22). Can you identify with any of these people?

2. What gifts within you are waiting to be born? Or can you be the midwife for someone else's infant gift?

Chapter 10

Mission

The church's mission is to follow Jesus in his life, death, and resurrection. Not only are individual Christians to model themselves after Christ, but the church is to be Christ in the world. In 1 Corinthians 12 and Ephesians 4, Paul writes of the church as the body of Christ. Throughout the epistles, the church is seen as sharing the life of Christ. Paul expects the church to do as Christ did, even experiencing suffering, death, and resurrection as Jesus did. 1 Peter 2:21 states, "For to this you have been called, because Christ also suffered for you, leaving you an example, that you should follow in his steps" (RSV). The church is to practice humility as Jesus did, taking the form of a servant (Phil. 2:5-11), rather than lording it over others.

In the Gospels, Jesus' disciples share both the mission and the destiny of Jesus. In Mark 8:31—10:52, three times Jesus tells the disciples that the Son of man must suffer many things, be killed, and rise again. Immediately afterward, three times, comes the message to the disciples. Take up your cross and follow me. Lose your life for my sake. Receive me as a child does. Be the servant of all. Give up all claim to status. Do not lord it over others. Give up your claim to power. John H. Yoder has written in *The Politics of Jesus,* "To follow after Christ is not simply to learn from him, but also to share his destiny."[1]

Just as Jesus' mission was not only for the apostles, those who had already decided to follow him, so our mission reaches out beyond the circle of the church. The church shares in the ministry of Christ. George W. Webber has written,

> In heeding the call of Christ, as we have seen, the Christian accepts a new vocation. The church and all its members exist, are called into being, in order to enter into the ministry of Christ in and for the world. The church is to be recognized by its missionary character—by the extent to which it reflects the fact that it is God's church and has accepted the mission he has assigned it.[5]

The Mission of Healing

The church begins its mission by following Jesus in his life, in his ministry to the suffering, the outcasts, the poor, and the powerless. In the Gospels, the activities of Jesus at which the Jewish leaders took the most offense were his healing on the Sabbath and his eating with tax collectors (the Roman collaborators) and sinners. It was not his calling together a band of disciples and teaching them that gave offense. It was his offering of healing and acceptance to the sick, to women, to children, to Gentiles and Samaritans that set Jesus apart from the other itinerant rabbis of his day. After the resurrection, Jesus not only told Peter to "feed my sheep" (John 21:17), but told all the disciples, "As the Father has sent me, even so I send you" (John 20:21). The church's mission is not only that of internal nurture, but to continue the entire ministry of Jesus, to which we also have been commissioned.

That ministry is being discovered in thousands of house churches, or basic ecclesial communities, as they are called in Latin America. In Latin America, these communities are primarily communities of the poor. In these house churches, the poor and powerless find solidarity in their suffering and find strength to work for justice. In standing together, they are able to persevere in spite of large landowners who try to take over the fields of small farmers. Alvaro Barreiro of Brazil has written,

> God's plan of salvation, revealed definitively in Jesus Christ, continues to be manifested and concretized historically as salvation and liberation, mercy and consolation for the poor and unfortunate, so long as the Church, the messianic people and the sacrament of salvation, moved by the Spirit of the Lord, performs acts and signs of justice, mercy, and love toward those who have nothing to eat or wear, or no place to live, and toward all the indigent, oppressed, and unfortunate, whether they be its members because of faith and baptism, or are beyond its visible borders. This is what is happening at present in thousands of CEBs [basic ecclesial communities] scattered over the length and breadth of [Brazil]. The poor Christians who comprise them live on faith and hope in the coming of the Kingdom, struggling with the poor but always efficacious resources of the gospel to overcome the state of dependence, oppression, and even misery in which they find themselves. The Church, which they are, effectively manifests the presence of the Kingdom among human beings when the poor, the dispossessed, and abandoned people of those communities are received in the Church as if it were their own home; when the poor who comprise those communities become conscious of the fact that they are the children of the Kingdom, a Kingdom of truth and justice, love and peace; and when those poor people, accepting the good news, are prompted by faith, hope, and love to perform concrete deeds and acts of justice, liberation, and salvation.[3]

But how do middle-class people, those with privilege, carry on this ministry of Jesus to the dispossessed? By standing with the suffering, the outcasts, the poor. By taking the side of the powerless. Some of these people are overseas. Many of them are in our own land, in cities, in rural areas, in small towns—the poor, those cheated out of a chance for a job or a decent place to live, minorities who have less of a chance because of the color of their skin, refugees without visas, women who have less of a chance because of their gender. They are especially children, who, whether or not they are poor, are generally powerless. Even if we find no others who need justice and healing, we can minister to our children, for whom Jesus was not too busy.

House churches in North America have found missions in sponsoring refugees, in sponsoring voluntary service units, in housing rehabilitation for the poor and elderly, in peace education. The Jubilee Fellowship in Philadelphia employs two part-time neighborhood ministers. One works with local and citywide groups on justice and economic development. Another neighborhood minister works with poor folks—ex-mental patients, disabled people, and the like—who eat at a local soup kitchen.

The church finds ways to minister to suffering and powerless people most easily by knowing them. A friend of mine in Chicago was asked how she found the energy and desire to work in an organization that seeks to build connections between people in North America and people overseas, especially the Philippines. She responded, "These people are my friends." She had worked with the church in the Philippines. She lives near Filipino and Hispanic neighbors now. She serves not only out of the principle, but out of friendship. Elizabeth O'Connor has written of the need for personal contact in the mission of justice and healing:

> It is simply not enough to be aware of the injustices of society. The contrast between what we have and what others have may stir conflict in us, but it will not be easily resolved. If we are to

do anything about injustices, we must feel them, and face the fact that it is painful to feel. We cannot keep protecting ourselves from sights and smells and sounds that are disturbing. We are not going to become truly radicalized until we get close enough to the oppressed to hear their groans and see their plight. . . .

The people I know who have made any radical shift in the way they live have had some exposure to poverty on a consistent basis. When the crossing is made from the world of the elite to that vast world of the poor, they cease to see their work as sacrificial. They begin to care about different things, to acquire a whole new set of values. They are doing what they most want to do. Life has meaning because they feel themselves to be engaged in the important struggles, and along the way they win a friend here and there who is in the same struggle, and soon they have a community.[4]

Often finding a mission to those who are powerless or in need of healing in spirit or body is not a matter of searching them out, but of offering God's life and Spirit to those whom we encounter. Once we put ourselves in a place where we can see the poor near us, then we no longer have to wonder who are our neighbors. They are there beside us. Then it becomes easier to change from seeing those neighbors as "them" to seeing neighbors as "us." It is no longer we helping them, but we together working for God's justice, peace, and wholeness in individual lives and in society.

When we are in the we-they way of thinking, it is easy to separate service from evangelism, to minister to people's needs in a one-up position that says: We are different from you. We are the helpers. You are the helpees. We sometimes come to this way of thinking by trying to avoid making "rice Christians." We don't want to require church attendance, for example, before we will help someone in need. Rightly, we want to help all in need, regardless of whether they become a part of the church. But in avoiding falling off that side of the boat, we have fallen off the other side. We have served without inviting people into the church. We have communicated that these people can receive our help, but they cannot be part of our community.

In one black community in the South, white Mennonites had served for thirty years, working for racial justice, demonstrating their belief in equality, but without trying, for most of those years, to establish a church. At the end of that time, a black Mennonite visited the community to interview a number of the people who had been served. Upon his identifying himself as a Mennonite, one woman's response to him was hearty laughter. The message Mennonites had unintentionally communicated was, You can be served by us, but you are not a part of us.

Part of the ministry of Christ is inviting people into the new community where there is neither Jew nor Greek, slave nor free, male nor female. In that community Christ has broken down the dividing walls between us and reconciled us both to God in one body (Eph. 4:14-17).

The Call to Mission

As house churches, we cannot be in mission everywhere at once. Jesus did not heal every sick person in Palestine. Neither can we minister to every person in need. Nor should we feel guilty because we do not. If God can work through the limitations of humanness, then we also should be willing to do so. What we need to do is to discover our call to mission and act according to that call. Otherwise we become what George Webber has called "promiscuous do-gooders," seeking to love and care for everybody in a way that ends up being superficial and insignificant. Instead, Webber has written, we can be freed to ask, "Among all the good things that need to be done, what is the good that it is your business to undertake; that is, for which you have the resources, time, talent, and energy in order to make a difference?"[5] Once we discover our particular call to mission, then we are free to say no to those good things that are not our calling. We are also freer than before to say yes to what is our calling because we can now focus our energy instead of dissipating it in many directions.

One method we have used to help people discover their God-given vocation, their calling, is the clearness meeting. The clearness meeting, as used by the Quakers, can help persons gain clearness about any decision. The person asking for clearness gathers several people—his or her house church plus one or two other significant people. The focus person prepares privately for the meeting and then begins the meeting by presenting the issue for which she is asking clearness. What is it that he brings to the new situation? What needs does she see? What abilities does he have? The process is very similar to that described in Chapter 9 on discerning gifts for ministry within the church. The idea behind the clearness meeting is that, in the house church or other small discerning group, people can best discover their vocation to mission as they listen to themselves, to others, and to God.

Robert C. Linthicum, pastor of the Presbyterian church in Grosse Pointe Woods, Michigan, has written:

> As serious Christians spend time in contemplation, worship, and study, and as they are supported and encouraged by others in their quest, they begin to uncover God's call to their outward journey. The call comes as the result of their serious deliberation on the question, What is it in which I am willing to invest my life? It rarely comes immediately and clearly, but only little by little. That call will fill them both with a sense of unease and

humility, because they will feel that the call is beyond them (which it should be; otherwise, there is no room for growth).[6]

Once people have discovered their particular calling and tested it in the church, they may then call others to test whether they, too, have been called to this ministry and will join them in serving God in this way. Or an entire house church may discern a particular ministry to do together. Even if a whole house church is not involved in a common mission, those who have a different calling can still stand with, and pray with, others in the church.

Is one's Christian vocation the same as one's occupation at which one earns a living? Not necessarily. People may choose to earn money at a job which is available and not always related to their calling. But we should not assume that the two are always separate. Elizabeth O'Connor has written in *The New Community*,[7] "To bear the new community's mark of commitment to the oppressed does not mean that the members will have to abandon their present callings, or betray their special gifts. What it does mean is the callings and gifts will be used for transforming the world."

Testing one's calling with the church and finding support in the church are resources for mission. Another resource for mission is prayer. Prayer not only guides us in finding direction for our mission. Prayer helps us continue in mission in spite of difficulties. Prayer and action are dependent on each other. Without action Christians will rust out. Without prayer we will burn out. Through prayer we sense the power of Christ's Spirit with us. Through prayer we are enabled to act in Christ's name. Prayer gives us that rest while we are working, of which Jesus spoke in Matthew 11:28-30 (RSV):

> Come to me, all who labor and are heavy laden, and I will give you rest. Take my yoke upon you, and learn from me; for I am

gentle and lowly in heart, and you will find rest for your souls. For my yoke is easy, and my burden is light.

Prayer can give us that rest, that calmness of spirit which allows us to continue in spite of the persecution which Jesus assured his followers would come.

Mission and the Way of the Cross

The earliest preaching of the apostles about Jesus focused on the cross and resurrection. In Peter's Pentecost sermon in Acts 2, in Paul's recounting of the story of Jesus delivered to him, in the hymn of the early church in Philippians 2:5-11, the important facts about Jesus are that he was killed, but God raised and exalted him. In Acts and the Epistles, nothing is said of his birth; little is said about his life. What is important, what determines people's response to Jesus as Christ, is how they respond to his death. The affirmation of the earliest preaching about Jesus is that this man Jesus, who was executed as a political criminal on a cross, is the exalted one of God. Jesus' death is not the end of the story. God has vindicated him. The apostles' preaching affirms that Jesus, the one who turned down the prerogatives of power when he was tempted in the wilderness, is the one to whom God has given ultimate power. This Jesus, who chose servanthood rather than lording it over others, is now Lord of all. This Jesus, who refused to use violence even in self-defense, is now the Victor.

Even the Gospels, from which we get our information about Jesus' birth and life, emphasize his death and resurrection to the extent that they have been called passion narratives with introductions.

That the cross is the turning point of Christian history is not often disputed. But the cross is not just something done for us 2,000 years ago. It is something we also are to do. Just as we are to follow Jesus in his ministry to the dispossessed, we are also to follow Jesus in the way of the cross.

Walking in the way of the cross is not just suffering an illness, or mourning the death of a loved one, or bearing the consequences of our own wrong actions, although we can be comforted that God understands our suffering in those times. But that is not the meaning of the cross. Walking in the way of the cross means living and risking death as Jesus did. It means giving up our rightful claims to power, possessions, status, and even life itself. It means standing up for peace and justice and shalom for all peoples in spite of the consequences. Walking in the way of the cross means giving up our fear of death. It means giving up our anxiety over whether we will lose money by being faithful to Christ. It means loving others indiscriminately, as Christ did, even loving our enemies.

So to take on Christ's mission in the world is to take risks. When we stand with and stand up for powerless and hurting people, we will sometimes suffer the consequences. Jesus was accused of having a demon for teaching that God has sent him and for healing on the Sabbath (John 7:20). So we should not be surprised if people make accusations against us for siding with the oppressed or for acting on the side of peace and justice.

The good news, however, is that Jesus did not expect his disciples to risk alone. He kept telling them, "Be not afraid. I am with you." Without fear, violence cannot control us. Without fear that others will take away what I have, I am free to act in spite of the risk to myself.

Not only is the Spirit of Christ with us, but the church is with us. It is one of the advantages of the house church that it can be more fully supportive of those who take risks for the sake of Christ's mission. I have seen a few large churches take such risks, but the larger the church, the more difficult it is to come to the unity of mind. More often, it is the small church which is willing to take gospel risks. One reason for this may be that with fewer people it simply takes less time to come to a decision. But I think another reason is that people in a small church know and trust each other better. They are more willing to trust the call of one of their members and more willing to hold him or her accountable. Because relationships are closer, they are better able to give support to that person in times of discouragement and difficulty.

Much has been written about the negative effects of groups on individual willingness to risk. Often the group mind is thought of as diluting the creativity of the individual. But a group, a house church, can also encourage the individual to greater creativity and risk. Because the church stands together in mission, it can support those who work for change. The church can encourage people to walk in the way of the cross.

Mission and Resurrection

The way of the cross is also the way of resurrection. Second Timothy 2:11-12 promises, "If we have died with him, we shall also live with him; if we endure, we shall also reign with him" (RSV). The way of suffering is the way to truth and life. Without risk and suffering, we learn little: When we invest our whole selves in the mission of Christ, we learn of the pain of the oppressed, but we also learn of their joys, the truths they see to which the powerful are blind. Instead of the loneliness of those who are self-sufficient, we find in standing with the powerless the joy of community. We discover the strength of responding with love rather than violence. We realize the power of the powerless. Through suffering and identification with those who are suffering, we find new life.

We come to our mission expecting only to help others. We find that we ourselves are helped. We grow in ways we had never anticipated. We find strengths we did not know we had.

The people of Church of the Saviour in Washington, D.C., have said that, when an authentic call of God comes to us, it will come as incredibly good news. Our call to take on the mission of Christ is not a burdensome task to which we need to push ourselves, but a joyful opportunity to share in the life of the risen Christ. As we take up the cross of Christ, we find Christ's presence in a new way in the band of people who have committed themselves to be Christ's presence in the world—the church.

Reflection and Action

1. In what ways have you been exposed to those who are suffering: the poor, victims of injustice, the sick, the outcasts of society, children, women, racial minorities, and so on? How has knowing these people affected your ability to respond to human need?

2. What is your Christian calling? How can you be involved in the mission of Christ? Or, what help do you need from the church in finding your calling?

3. What is the mission of your church? How can it better show the presence of Christ in the world?

Chapter 11

Growing

If house churches survive, they grow. They may or may not grow larger. They may or may not give birth to new house churches. But they do not stay the same. New people come. Some of the founders move to a different city. Even if the same people are here that were here in the beginning, they are not the same. They are older. They are dealing with new issues in their lives. Part of being the church is learning to manage change and growth.

The first change which most house churches experience is adding new people. People become an active part of house churches in stages. Once the initial group forms, members who are successfully added later on follow a predictable path of entry into the church.

The first question which the new person needs to have answered is, Am I in? Do I belong? In small churches that expect a high level of commitment, new people can sometimes find it hard to break in. A close group that has been together for a long time can find it hard to include someone new. The group has its traditions, its own vocabulary, its songs, its habits. Each new person added to the group brings the possibility of change, and change can be threatening.

House churches can welcome new people joyfully without

diluting their commitment levels by paying attention to the messages—usually nonverbal—which they give to newcomers. The welcoming church will greet new persons and include them in conversations. The church can provide songbooks or song sheets to all music, so that newcomers can participate in the singing. Church members can listen to the new person to hear their stories, needs, wants, and fears.

Mennonite Church of the Servant has newcomers' classes where people who have recently started coming to our church can be initiated into the traditions, structures, and theology of our church. In six weekly sessions, we discuss various aspects of the church's covenant: the spiritual journey, friendship with God and the journey inward, our journey together as a church (or history, our organizational structures, our reasons for (doing things as we do), the way of the cross and mission in the world, and how a new person can affirm the covenant of our church.

Other churches have had separate house churches for nurture and outreach. Nurture groups are more stable and are freed to go beyond the basics of the faith. Outreach groups are more open to new people and more attractive to those who would like to join a house church in which they are not the only new people.

All these things are simply ways of telling the newcomer, "You are in. We want you to belong to our 'family.' "

Newcomers also ask, Do I count? How can I be of use in this group? Does what I say or do make any difference? What can I say or do? Often churches ask this question too soon. If they are eager for someone to take on a particular task, they may ask the newcomer right away to take on a role in the church. To the newcomer, this may seem like asking for commitment and accountability before he or she has really been included in the church. Other churches wait too long to help the new person be of use in the church. Then the newcomer may decide that she is not needed here. Once the newcomer is no longer a visitor, once he belongs, then the appropriate next step is to find a task for that person to do, to find one or more gifts that person has to offer the church and which the church needs. Only then do new persons ask, Am I loved? Does this church like me? And the church asks, Do you love us? Then we build the ties of relationship. We ask for emotional attachment to each other only after the questions of identification and accountability have been settled.[1]

If a house church wants to bring new people into the church, however, the most important task is to decide that that is what it wants to happen. The church that is not intentional about being welcoming to new people will probably add a few people over the years, but will tend to stabilize at a number that feels comfortable. To grow beyond that number requires a decision and the willingness to keep the door of the house church open for whomever God sends our way.

Mobility

House churches in urban areas especially have no lack of opportunity for experiencing change. The average North American moves once every eighteen months, and many of those moves are from one city to another. During the three years I was in seminary and away from Mennonite Church of the Servant, the number of participants increased slightly, but only about half of them were people who had been part of the church before I left. Others in the church, like me, have been in Wichita, then left, and later returned. Of the original twenty people who saw the beginnings of the church nine years ago, only three have lived in Wichita that entire time.

That kind of mobility can be frustrating to a small church. The second year of the existence of Mennonite Church of the Servant, over half of the Sunday morning house church left, almost all of them moving out of town. The effect would have been devastating to the house church had it not had the support of the other house church in Mennonite Church of the Servant, which sent some of its members to the morning house church to boost their numbers and morale. The smaller the church, the closer the relationships, and the more we mourn the loss of people who leave the church.

One response to this mobility is to encourage people not to move. Some churches have asked for commitment to the church over commitment to job and have interpreted that to mean that church members are encouraged to find employment where they can continue to be a part of this particular church. That can be an appropriate request. Churches, especially small churches, need some continuity in order simply to survive. Some leaders and others in the church will want to make that kind of commitment because the church needs them and/or they need the church.

Another response is to see mobility as opportunity rather than as crisis. While we can encourage some people to stay rather than move with a job, we can hardly turn back the tide of mobility in an age when almost 90 percent of Americans are employees, rather than working for themselves. I prefer to see the people leaving our church for employment elsewhere as students who have been learning something new about what it means to be the church and are now taking that experience with them into a new situation.

Many people who have been a part of us for two or three years have learned much about house churches and how much more commitment to the church is possible than they had thought previously. They have tested new leadership skills in house churches and have found that they are capable of being shepherds or taking on other roles which most churches reserve for those who are over forty. So instead of trying to make them feel guilty for leaving, I look on them as people who have received a house-church education and I commission them to teach others wherever they go. In some cases, people may be moving to where there is no church that will meet their needs in theology or commitment. So we can encourage them and support them in starting a new house church. Then we can send them forth with joy and not just mourn our loss.

Stages of Group Life

Not only does the membership of house churches change, but the church itself changes as it grows older. Richard Rohr, pastor of the New Jerusalem Community in Cincinnati, Ohio, has written of four stages in the life of any group built on trust.[2]

The first stage is the honeymoon stage. It is the stage of wonder, excitement about new life together, and dreams of what might be. This is the beginning of love; only in this stage, we are not in love with a real group of people, but in love with the dream. Rohr has commented:

> Fortunately or unfortunately we do not usually know that we are in stage one. We are probably not aware that community is about to happen. We are uniquely in the power of the Spirit. It is usually unprogrammed, unplanned, and unsuspected. It is usually pure gift. Only years later do we become aware of the power available and given at the beginning.

> We cannot maintain the fervor and euphoria of stage one for very long. If we try—as many groups do—we will pay a very high price: blindness. It is a great and very subtle temptation precisely because stage one appears to be so holy, inspired, and empowered. It is not unlike the first blush of romantic love, and no one wants to let go of it. . . .

> We lean on them [the group] heavily, because we are drawing

life from them and they are putting us in touch with the depths of our own dreaming.[3]

In stage two of group life we experience conflict. The church has not fulfilled all our dreams. We find that the "community is imperfect. And so is the leader, the vision, the structure, the timing, the theology, the initial call, the present situation, and the tuna casserole that was served for lunch." Stage two, Rohr has said, is a time of nonlistening to others, to God, and even to ourselves. In this stage many house churches dissolve or individuals leave. Or they retreat into stage one rather than venture into this great and terrible wilderness.

The way through this wilderness is through competent spiritual direction from people who have been this way before and know how to pass through the darkness into the light. In stage two we realize our own inadequacy and our need and realize that we have to be converted in order to live. "It is a letting-go of control, and this is what we do not want to do."

Only in stage three does love really begin. "We still know everything that we knew in stage two. We know that we live in an imperfect world and with an imperfect self, but we are freed to love anyway." In stage three we are free to deal with real issues and not just projections, fears, and reactions.

> Stage-three people are the creators of community. Their very freedom draws life around them. They seem to draw their life from within themselves and are, in this sense, healthily independent. They do not really need community, it appears. And yet they decide for what God has decided for. They choose to participate, to share in the pain and life of God for the sake of God's kingdom. They know that they do not *have* to do this, and yet they *must* do it to be who they already are.

> You must have one—hopefully several—stage-three people in

order to form a community. Sometimes, like Moses and Miriam, they are themselves formed on the same journey that they are leading. These are the sisters and brothers who can say to us floundering around in stages one and two, "I have been here before. Come, let's walk together."[4]

Stage four is the goal toward which we move: the stage of clear vocation. In stage four, we listen, we respond, we love. "Stage-four communities come not to do their own will, but the will of the One who sends them. They are the clearest incarnation of Jesus in time and space." Stage-one people think they are in stage four. But the unity of stage four is not that of unrealized dreams. By their time and trials together, stage-four churches have discovered a basis for unity deeper than momentary differences or similarities. They are taking up God's mission in the world.

Multiplying by Dividing

What if a house church grows beyond twelve or fifteen people? Is it no longer a house church? What has happened to the benefits of a living-room-sized church? The answer is to multiply the church by dividing.

Within the first year of existence of Mennonite Church of the Servant, we divided into two house churches. The process was painful for some of us. Some were afraid of cutting off relationships with those in the other house church. But with too large a church, close relationships could not have remained as they were in the beginning. As a whole church, we went on a weekend retreat, and by Saturday afternoon we had come to consensus on dividing into two house churches and had amicably decided how to do the division.

It was important for us to do that dividing soon. The longer we waited, the harder it would have been to separate into two house churches. What made the division palatable to most of the church was the scheduling of regular meetings of the whole church. We retained our corporate identity as Mennonite Church of the Servant for the whole church and chose new names for each of the house churches. We tried to keep the advantages of a house church and the advantages of being a little bit larger with more resources for music and worship planning and more peers for singles, marrieds, and children. Nevertheless, division always has some pain, but it is the necessary pain of growth. To avoid that pain is to stagnate.

John W. Miller of the Kitchener-Waterloo (Ont.) House Churches has written of the process of multiplying by dividing in one of their house churches:

> The last subdivision of this kind that I experienced was an especially difficult one. But now that it is over, we are also beginning to see that the difficulties were necessary in helping us rediscover old truths that we were in danger of forgetting.
>
> Some in our church had become too invested in this particular group of people. The very stability and warmth of house church experience had given them new confidence, but also inhibited them from growing in other ways with other people equally important to their well-being.
>
> Leadership had been slowly ripening in our midst, but we might have missed it were it not for the crisis of dividing. Contrary to our initial thoughts the new group would have someone to lead it after all! The recognition and affirmation of this fact was a moving experience.
>
> A house church cannot be built on human friendship alone. We knew this, but when it came to deciding how to divide, "compatibility" became a big concept. Only when we recognized once again that our house church calling "in Christ" is to grow

in our capacity to love everyone, did we find the right way ahead.

God's providence and prayer also became more real to us again in the midst of this experience. At one point we were ready to give up and stay together, even though we knew we were suffering from bigness. Then we were suddenly confronted by conflicting schedules. We could no longer find an acceptable meeting night. This forced us to think new thoughts and pray with new intensity that God would lead us. Unity came in a meeting where we gathered with a special sense of surrender and prayer.[5]

In Mennonite Church of the Servant we now have five house churches. Each house church meets weekly at a time of its own choosing. The whole church meets twice a month on Sunday morning for worship (called "the Gathering") and once a month for decision-making (the church life meeting). As a whole church we handle finances, hire staff, do long-range planning, create our own songbook, and relate to other churches and conferences. Each house church chooses its own name. It chooses its own shepherd or shepherds, but these need to be affirmed by the whole church.

Shepherds of all the house churches meet regularly to discuss matters that concern the whole church, or issues within house churches on which other shepherds or the whole church might provide guidance. Shepherds bring up the names of visitors to the Gathering and suggest which house church might take responsibility for follow-up. As a whole church, we plan Christian education activities for children. Social activities happen both as a whole church and as house churches. House churches or the whole church can celebrate communion.

We have tried to retain the benefits of smallness while still providing some of the services of the larger church: more of a peer group for children, the flexibility of being able to switch from one house church to another without leaving the church entirely, the ability to use the gifts of teaching or music or administration of persons in other house churches, a larger worship service that allows people to be on the edge of the church while they are still deciding whether they want to belong.

By the house churches' meeting weekly and the Gathering only twice a month, however, we have tried to indicate the priority of the house church. For us, the house church is not an optional extra. It is a vital part of being the church. It is the most important place where we are church to each other.

Some churches larger than we, who value the house church model, have subdivided even further. The Church of the Saviour in Washington, D.C., now has six faith communities within it and smaller mission groups within those communities. The Assembly, Goshen, Indiana, has two clusters of small groups which meet as clusters weekly and together once every seven weeks. Reba Place Fellowship in Evanston, Illinois, also has three clusters of from thirty to fifty people within the larger church.

Virgil Vogt, an elder at Reba Place, wrote,

> As the church continued to grow, we finally reached the point where something had to be done about size. Should we form two churches, or decentralize within a single church? We decided to remain together as one church, but formed three small groups operating as sub-units within the congregation. Because of the strong "house-church" vision at Reba, we pictured these as house-churches, giving them a great deal of authority and pastoral function. In our zeal to empower the smaller groups, we swung too far in a decentralized direction. But with a couple of years experience, and some re-balancing in favor of the central congregation, we had a format that worked well for many years. . . .

A decade came and went, while the church continued to grow. Gradually, however, many of us began to realize that a significant loss of function was occurring in relationship to the total congregation. By this time we numbered about 150 members; with children and other seekers and friends, the total group included more than 300 persons.

In relationship to the activities of the entire congregation, a growing number of Reba members felt somewhat disinterested, somewhat uninvolved or distant, in some cases even alienated and frustrated.... There were many significant relationships and meanings carried by this larger group. But these functions have size limitations. As the number of extended relationships became more numerous, it was increasingly difficult to sustain the same quality or sense of closeness that was present in earlier times.

Again we faced the question of what to do about size. Should we form two separate congregations, or continue in some way as one church?

As we prayerfully considered this question, it seemed clear that we should stay together as one large congregation. In order to do this, however, we decided to form a third intermediate level of church life, transferring many of the functions of the total congregation to this middle level. In this way we have sought to recreate the values which we experienced when we were a congregation of 30-50 members.

Now we have three "clusters" within the framework of Reba Place Church. Each cluster includes several small groups which function in much the same way that small groups have functioned her over the years. But now, most of the pastoral leadership, pastoral decisions, picnics, work-days, child-care, extended family relationships, leadership development and handling of crises, are all organized at the cluster level, rather than at the all-church level. . . .

The change hasn't been easy. And not everyone is fully satisfied with the present three-tiered church. . . . Some find this too large and complex. . . . Our hope is that the present arrangement will help us meet requirements for both quantity and quality. We are called to grow and evangelize. We are also called to develop strong, covenant relationships which express what it means to be the household of faith. With God's help we want to live out this calling in a faithful and productive manner.[6]

An alternative to clustering that does not require as much structure is simply to start another church. One assembly of house churches could divide into two smaller assemblies of house churches. Or a single house church could be started with some members from the older congregation. The advantage of this model is that it does not require as many layers of organization and is more practical when there is some distance between the older and younger church. A new house church in the same city with an older house church might still decide to do some activities (for example, children's Christian education) with the parent congregation.

There is no one structure that will fit all house churches or clusters of house churches. The structure that fits best will be related to size, the experience of the members, and other factors. One characteristic of house churches is their adaptability, their willingness to pioneer in creating new structures for the new situation. The desire to maintain the closeness of the house church has been the motivating factor in that creativity in finding ways to be house churches and continue to grow.

None of our structures are absolute. They can change as needs change. Whether we have two or three layers of organization is not the most important matter. That depends on our situation. What takes priority in our structures is the basic level of the church: the house church. Unless we build on that foundation of caring, sharing, discipling, worship, teaching, and serving, our other structures will not shelter us.

Connecting

Whether churches consist of one house church or are a group of clusters of house churches, they need connections with other churches. All the gifts necessary for ministry in the local church are not present in one person; neither are all the gifts necessary for the total church's ministry present in one congregation. The smaller the church, the more necessary are connections with other churches.

These connections are happening in a variety of ways. Many of the churches which include intentional communities have formed their own covenanted networks: the Shalom Covenant Communities, of which Reba Place Fellowship is a part, and the Community of Communities are examples. House churches have scheduled retreats at church campgrounds with other house churches in their region of the continent. In central Kansas, a small group of house churches has been getting together for common worship on an occasional basis.

The Community House Church in Washington, D.C., has begun a fraternal relationship with the Eighth Day Faith Community of the Church of the Saviour. The Community House Church reported, "We will worship with them about once every six weeks and see what specifics develop out of getting to know one another. A basic reason for this is to help end our feelings of being small and off in our own little corner of D.C., by being connected to something bigger, older, and a bit more institutional than we are."

The House Church newsletter, published in Newton, Kansas, has sought since 1978 to provide a link among house churches of many traditions. Many house churches also have connections with the denominations in which many of their members have ties. In this way house churches can draw on the resources of the larger church as well as provide a witness to the larger church of a different style of church life.

We need these connections with each other as we deal with change.

Philip Martin of the Kitchener-Waterloo House Churches has expressed well our attitude toward change in his poem "New Wineskins":

> The goal to which our forms move
> is not perfection
> or beauty
> or comfort
> but toward the death
> through which our forms
> break
> and emerge into
> new and unimaginable
> life.
> Let us not despise
> perfection
> or beauty
> or even comfort
> for we must love our forms
> if they are to begin
> speaking to us.
> But in the maturing of love
> we need to learn
> letting go—
> the release of the Spirit
> through our forms
> into cracking. [7]

Reflection and Action

1. How does your church welcome new people? How are you a welcoming person?

2. What stages of group life have you experienced? In what stage is your house church or small group now?

3. If you could structure the church in the way that best fits your situation, how would it look? Toward what goal should your church be aiming?

Chapter 12

Beginning

How does a house church begin? A house church begins when "two or three are gathered together in my name" ready to be the body of Christ (Matt. 18:20). More important than any structure or technique is their intention to be the church, their willingness to exhibit all the marks of the church.

If a house church is beginning as a totally new congregation, the group will find it helpful to decide on its identity. Is this the church? Does the group want to be the body of Christ? David Habegger has written about what it means to be the church:

> To be a church is more than being a Christian sharing group. It is to be a group of persons mutually committed to following Christ, to searching for the mind of Christ, to being open to the leading of the Spirit in all things. As a group they will engage in worship, study, witness, service, and fellowship. They will seek to be open to each other, to be supportive in healthy ways, and to share their resources of presence, time, gifts, and other resources. The group will celebrate the Lord's Supper, and when there are new commitments to Christ, baptism.[1]

In other words, a house church begins when a group of people decides that it wants to do what is essential to being the church. A new house church does not have to have a Sunday school and a mission committee or meet on Sunday morning in order to be the church. What is essential is a commitment to Christ and to discipling each other in the way of Christ through worship, teaching, sharing, deciding, and mission.

Once a group has decided it wants to be Christ's church, it may be well for them to decide on some kind of statement of the purpose of their group, a preliminary covenant. This may be no more than a commitment to follow Christ, or it may be a fuller covenant setting forth the faith and expectations of the church that the members can already affirm together.

If the church wishes, it can then ask for denominational recognition, if that is possible and desired by the church.

House Churches Within an Existing Congregation

Sometimes house churches do not start from scratch. They come into being as a larger congregation sees a vision for smaller groupings within the church and decides to begin several house churches. This can be done and has been done, but it has its own set of difficulties. While the new independent house church takes greater risks from the mobility of its members and the fragility of new structures, house churches newly created within an existing congregation take the risk of not being accepted as "real" churches by many members of the larger congregation. If the larger congregation already has a complex set of structures and programs, committees and boards, the house churches may be seen as simply one more layer of structure to carry on some limited set of functions in the church, such as fellowship and pastoral care. Or house churches may be viewed with a sense of threat by those within the congregation who see the change as a message that what was happening before was not good.

I will not pretend to offer a sure formula for how to start house churches within an existing congregation. But following are some considerations for those interested in forming house churches.

People in an existing congregation will accept new house churches more easily when house churches are seen as an answer to a pressing need. The church that says, "Something has got to happen. Too many people are falling between the cracks," has a better chance at success with house churches than the congregation in which everything seems to be going smoothly and the house church is seen as an additional program of the church. New life and radical change come out of a sense of death and suffering, not when things are going well. Only the sick have need of a physician.

To begin house churches means a clear change in business as usual. People and churches do not make radical changes except under pressure or pain of some kind. If a congregation is able to bring its pain into the open, talk about its weaknesses, and be open to alternatives for the future, then house churches may be an alternative which can bring healing and new life.

To start house churches in a congregation where none have been before is threatening because it implies that what has been could be improved. To those who do not want to deal with problems and pain, house churches seem like an un-wanted criticism of the past. To some extent, any change or improvement is a criticism of what has been. But a change need not imply that the former was never good. It may simply mean that new situations demand new responses. We can celebrate the beginnings of our congregation and still be ready to move on to new structures that better serve the current needs.

To be the church to each other in a house church implies a strong commitment in time and emotional energy. If members of house churches are to give themselves fully to the business of being a house church, that may mean that the larger church will need to cut back on the number of committee meetings and other activities in which people have been involved. The larger church may need to take some activities that it has sponsored and turn them over entirely to the house churches. Adult Christian education, for example, can happen in house churches probably more effectively and certainly more flexibly than in Sunday morning classes of 45 to 50 minutes. Pastoral care can take on a new dimension if it is done in house churches or by shepherds of house churches rather than only by the pastor or a small committee within the larger church. Then the pastor's role will be less that of giving direct pastoral care, than of training shepherds for pastoral care and coordinating the pastoral care of people on the fringe of the church. If the larger church turns over some major functions of the church totally to the house churches, they stand a better chance of being taken seriously by the churches as a whole. If not, the message that comes across is, "House churches are not essential to the functioning of this congregation; they are just an addition to the church activities that you can take or leave." It is better to give the message, "House churches are free to be the church."

Clarify what activities will happen in the larger church and what will happen in the house churches. This can sometimes be divided on the basis of what each size group does best. Choirs and big musical events happen best in a large group. Discipling people who are struggling with moral issues happens best in a small group. Some activities such as prayer can be done well, but differently, in both small and large churches.

Decide on the relationship of house church membership to membership in the larger church. Will membership in a house church be a requirement for membership in the larger church? Will all members be encouraged to be part of house churches? Or will house churches be simply accepted or tolerated as an option for those who want them? It is possible for any of these three choices to work, but the church should choose which will be its attitude toward the new house churches.

Requiring membership in house churches will be difficult for most existing churches. Unless the church has consensus on this step, one cannot suddenly change the basis for membership in the congregation, or longtime members who do not want to be part of house churches will feel betrayed.

What will probably work better for the success of house churches is to make them completely voluntary and allow people to choose which house church they want to be a part of. But encourage people to join house churches and, in fact, expect that current members and new members will want to be part of house churches because that is where so much of the church life is happening. This leaves some flexibility to deal with the exceptions: the elderly person who is homebound, the missionary or voluntary service worker who is serving overseas but wants to maintain church ties back home, the person who wants a one-year sabbatical from the intensity of house church life, the person who wants to switch to a new house church and is still in transition.

Do not be afraid to spend time processing the decision to start house churches. Any time you spend now in reaching agreement over house churches will be saved later on when the house churches are actually operating. The person who is now so opposed to house churches may be able to view them more favorably when he or she is convinced that you are listening and will take his or her objections seriously. If you simply ignore that person now, you run the risk of sabotage or noncooperation later on. No house church can begin with enthusiasm when one or more members have come with an attitude of "I said this wouldn't work." Take your time and give the Spirit time to work in people's hearts.

What Does a New House Church Do?

Begin right away with being the church. Worship. Share with each other. Pray together. Have fun together. Eat together. Don't wait until you are larger to begin being the church. A church does not have to wait until there are twenty people there. There is no magic number. Neither paid pastors, nor buildings, nor a Sunday school, nor a choir, nor a piano, nor study guides, nor incorporation papers are necessary to being the church. Instead of waiting to become larger to be the church, be the church now with however many people are willing to commit themselves to this particular group being the body of Christ.

One good way to begin in your meetings together is by sharing spiritual pilgrimages with each other. This not only helps you learn to know one another better, it is also a way of sharing with each other what is important to you about your faith and what experiences you have had that have affected your faith. How have you come to faith? Where are you headed?

It is also helpful in the beginning to be clear about leadership. Who is leading the worship this evening? Who is responsible for finding some songsheets? Who will write up the covenant that we decided on this morning? Who will handle pastoral care needs? Who will handle contacts with denominational offices? Leadership decisions at this point can be temporary. You do not need to decide now on complex structures of leadership. But what minimal structures you do have need to be clear. Someone has to say, "Now it is time to begin (or end)."

Dreams and Visions

Share your visions for the future with each other, and dream new dreams for the church. This is stage one, the stage for dreaming. There is excitement about being part of something new, of letting new structures reflect something of you and your dreams. Now is a time for creativity, for brainstorming wild ideas and choosing which of those ideas might become reality.

Set goals. What does your house church want to be a year from now? Five years from now? Ten years from now? If your dreams came to reality, how would the church be functioning? What would people be doing? How would the church be structured? Is the house church a temporary stage on the way to being a sanctuary church, or is the house church your ideal form of the church? How large do you see your church getting before it divides and becomes two churches? What kind of leadership do you see as desirable? How will people be growing in their Christian faith?

Plan strategy. How will you get from where you are now to the goals that you want to come to reality? What is the first step? What is the next step? Who will do it? When? Be specific.

Pray about what the church should become and let the Spirit lead you. I see no necessary conflict between careful planning on our part and depending on the guidance of the Spirit. God expects us to do our part in cooperating with the divine way of doing things. At the same time, we recognize that all our ideas and plans are only partial reflections of the glory which God wishes to reveal through the church. We pray in that poverty of spirit that is willing to set aside all our carefully laid out goals and strategies when God shows us a new path toward new goals. We pray in the willingness to give up our own visions so that we can share in God's new vision for us.

Getting Help

New house churches do not have to do all this alone. Do not be afraid to connect with others who have already gone through the experience of becoming a church. Write, call, or go find people who can help you over the rough spots—people in other house churches or perhaps a denominational staff person with experience with house churches.

If you see that relationships within the house church are sick rather than healthy, don't ignore the problem, hoping it will go away. It won't. Talk about the problem in your house church, and get outside help, if necessary.

Visit other house churches, especially those that have been in existence for a number of years. They can give you a new perspective on the problems you know you have, and help you identify problems of which you were not aware.

Read books about house churches and church renewal. Read periodicals such as *The House Church* newsletter, *Sojourners*, *The Other Side*, and *Gathering: The Small Group Newsletter*. Go to house-church retreats, where you can talk with others who are now in house churches. Beginning with p. 169 is a list of printed resources that may help you learn from the experience of others in house-church related activities.

Do not be afraid. God is with you as you build the church.

Reflection and Action

1. If you are not now part of a house church and want to be, spend some time reflecting on what barriers are keeping you from helping to form the church. What can you do to remove—or go around—those barriers?

2. What is your next step? Are you willing to let the Spirit lead you even though you do not see very far ahead?

3. If you are thinking about house churches within your existing congregation, what should be your first step? What would the house churches do that the church is not doing now? What would the house churches do that the larger church is currently doing? What pressing need of your congregation would be met by creating house churches?

Notes

Chapter 1

1. Grand Rapids, Mich.: Eerdmans, 1980, p. 38.

2. Floyd V. Filson, "The Significance of the Early House Churches," *Journal of Biblical Literature* 58 (1939), p. 107.

3. In "A Brief History of the House Church, *The House Church* 1:2 (Dec. 1978), pp. 1-2.

4. Walter Klaassen, ed., *Anabaptism in Outline* (Scottdale, Pa.: Herald Press, 1981), p. 124.

5. "Church Order for Members of Christ's Body, Arranged in Seven Articles by Leopold Scharnschlager," *Mennonite Quarterly Review* 38:4 (October 1964), p. 354.

6. Michael Skinner, *House Groups* (London: Epworth Press and SPCK, 1969), p. 105.

7. New York: Morehouse-Gorham Co., 1956.

8. Reprinted in *Concern*, no. 5 (June 1958), Mennonite Publishing House, Scottdale, Pa.

Chapter 2

1. See Benjamin Zablocki, *Alienation and Charisma* (New York: The Free Press, 1980), pp. 294-95.

2. Spencer Estabrooks, "Our Covenanting Process: Grain of Wheat Church-Community in Winnipeg," *The House Church* 6:1 (March 1983), pp. 1, 6-7.

Chapter 3

1. "Why We Worship," *The House Church* 2:3 (June 1979), p. 1.
2. Garden City, N.Y.: Doubleday, 1976, p. 269.
3. P. 86.

Chapter 4

1. Nashville: Abingdon, 1980, p. 38.
2. *With Open Hands* (Notre Dame, Ind.: Ave Maria Press, 1972), p. 147.
3. Pp. 31-32.
4. P. 40.

Chapter 5

1. Ruth Klaassen, "Socialization of Production and Reproduction," *The House Church* 4:6 (December 1981), p. 3.
2. Valley Forge: Judson Press, 1979.
3. Newton, Kans.: Faith and Life Press, 1982, p. 10.

Chapter 6

1. Downers Grove, Ill.: InterVarsity Press, 1982.

Chapter 7

1. Scottdale, Pa.: Herald Press, 1979, p. 14.
2. "Binding and Loosing," *Concern*, no. 14, pp. 30-31.
3. Valley Forge: Judson Press, 1982, p. 92.
4. *Interior Castle*, E. Allison Peers, trans. and ed. (Garden City, N.Y.: Doubleday, 1961), III.2, pp. 68-69. Used by permission of Doubleday & Company, Inc.
5. By the author, 1979. Reprinted in 1980 by Forward Movement Publications, Cincinnati, Ohio, p. 16.

Chapter 8

1. "Seeking Unity and Living with Our Differences," *Coming Together* 3:3 (June 1985), p. 1.
2. David Augsburger, unpublished paper, "Conflict, Confusion, Concord in Christian Community."

3. "Some Dimensions of the Quaker Decision-making Process," *Friends Journal*, May 15, 1982, p. 7.

4. Steere, p. 8.

5. Downers Grove, Ill.: InterVarsity Press, 1982, pp. 191ff.

6. "Basic Concepts About Decision Making, Fellowship of Hope, Elkhart, Indiana," *The House Church* 7:3 (September 1984), p. 8.

Chapter 9

1. "Opening Gifts in Cedar Falls," *The House Church* 5:2 (Spring, 1982), p. 4.

2. Rev. ed. (Newton, Kans.: Faith and Life Press, 1983).

3. Waco, Tex.: Word Books, 1971, p. 17.

4. "The Fullness of Christ: Perspectives on Ministries in Renewal," *Concern*, no. 17 (February 1969), pp. 33-93.

5. *Life Together*, John W. Doberstein, trans. (New York: Harper & Row, 1954), p. 94.

Chapter 10

1. (Grand Rapids, Mich.: Eerdmans, 1972), p. 128.

2. *The Congregation in Mission: Emerging Structures for the Church in an Urban World* (Nashville: Abingdon, 1964), p. 66.

3. *Basic Ecclesial Communities: The Evangelization of the Poor*, trans. by Barbara Campbell (Maryknoll, N.Y.: Orbis Books, 1982), pp. 52-53.

4. *The New Community* (New York: Harper & Row, 1976), p. 22.

5. *Today's Church: A Community of Exiles and Pilgrims* (Nashville: Abingdon, 1979), p. 95.

6. "Spiritual Gifts and the Journey Outward," *The House Church* 7:1 (March 1984), p. 2.

7. (New York: Harper & Row, 1976), p. 100.

Chapter 11

1. William C. Schutz, *The Interpersonal Underworld* (Palo Alto, Calif.: Science and Behavior Books, Inc., 1966), pp. 1-28, 168-88.

2. See his article "All of Life Together Is a Stage," *Sojourners* 10:2 (February 1981), pp. 17-19.

3. Rohr, p. 18.

4. Rohr, p. 19.

5. "Lessons Learned in Subdivision," *The House Church* 3:4 (September 1980), p. 1.

6. "Reba Place Church; Learning to Deal with Size," *The House Church* 6:3 (November 1983), pp. 1, 6-8.

7. *The House Church* 5:2 (Spring, 1982), p. 8.

Chapter 12

1. "Marks of a House Church," *The House Church* 2:1 (February 1979), p. 6.

More Resources
for House Churches

House Churches in General

Allen, Donald R. *Barefoot in the Church*. Richmond, Va.: John Knox Press, 1972.

Anderson, Philip and Phoebe. *The House Church*. Nashville: Abingdon Press, 1975. This book describes the house church as an encounter group within the larger congregation.

Barlow, T. Ed. *Congregational House Churches*. Independence, Mo.: Herald Publishing House, 1978. The author is a minister in the Reorganized Church of Latter Day Saints.

Carroll, Jackson W., ed. *Small Churches Are Beautiful*. San Francisco: Harper & Row, 1977.

Chicago Theological Seminary Register 61:2 (December 1970), 63:2 (February 1973), 64:1 (November 1973), 66:1 (Winter, 1976), entire issues.

Christianity and Crisis 41 (September 21, 1981), several articles.

Clark, Stephen B. *Building Christian Communities: Strategy for Renewing the Church*. Notre Dame, Ind.: Ave Maria Press, 1972.

Ellison, Henry Leopold. *The Household Church*. Exeter: Paternoster Press, 1967.

Foster, Arthur L., ed. *The House Church Evolving*. Chicago: Exploration Press, 1976.

Jackson, Dave. *Coming Together: All Those Communities and What They're Up To*. Minneapolis: Bethany Fellowship, 1978. On intentional communities.

Kraus, C. Norman. *The Community of the Spirit*. Grand Rapids, Mich.: William B. Eerdmans, 1974.

Lundin, Jack W. *A Church for an Open Future: Biblical Roots and Parish Renewal*. Philadelphia: Fortress Press, 1977. The story of the Community of Christ the Servant in west suburban Chicago.

O'Connor, Elizabeth. *Call to Commitment: The Story of the Church of the Saviour, Washington, D.C.* New York: Harper & Row, 1963.

O'Halloran, James. *Living Cells: Developing Small Christian Community*. Rev. ed. Maryknoll, N.Y.: Orbis Books, 1984. Draws on missionary experiences in Africa and Latin America.

Schramm, John, and Anderson, David. *Dance in the Steps of Change*. New York: Thomas Nelson, Inc., 1970. The story of the Community of Christ, an ecumenical church in Washington, D.C.

Skinner, Michael. *House Groups*. London: Epworth Press and SPCK, 1969.

Southcott, Ernest. *The Parish Comes Alive*. New York: Morehouse-Gorham Co., 1956.

Snyder, Harold A. *The Problem of Wineskins: Church Structures in a Technological Age*. Downers Grove, Ill.: InterVarsity Press, 1975. "The church is you who pray, not where you pray."

The Other Side. 13:2 (April 1977), entire issue.

The Rule of Taize, in French and in English. New York: The Seabury Press, 1968.

Thomas, Donald. *Manual for the Church in the Home*. Valley Forge: American Baptist Home Mission Societies, 1961.

Vanier, Jean. *Community and Growth: Our Pilgrimage Together*. New York: Paulist Press, 1979. This book grows out of the experiences of the L'Arche communities around the world, in which mentally handicapped and "normal" people live together in Christian community.

Vogt, Virgil. "Small Congregations." *Concern*, no. 5 (June 1958).

Weber, Hans-Ruedi. "The Church in the House." *Concern*, no. 5 (June 1958).

New Testament and Church History

Banks, Robert. *Paul's Idea of Community: The Early House Churches in Their Historical Setting*. Grand Rapids, Mich.: William B. Eerdmans Publishing Company, 1980.

Cullmann, Oscar. *Early Christian Worship*. London: SCM Press, 1969.

Davies, J. G. *Daily Life in the Early Church*. London: Lutterworth Press, 1952.

Filson, Floyd V. "The Significance of the Early House Churches." *Journal of Biblical Literature* 58 (1939):105-12.

Klauck, Hans-Josef. *Hausgemeinde und Hauskirche im fruehen Christentum.* Stuttgart: Verlag Katholisches Bibelwerk, 1981.

Rordorf, W. "Die Hausgemeinde der vorkonstantinischen Zeit." In Williams, C. W., ed. *Kirche: Tendenzen und Ausblicke.* Berlin: Gelnhausen, 1971. Pp. 190-96, 235-36.

House Churches Around the World

Barreiro, Alvaro. *Basic Ecclesial Communities: The Evangelization of the Poor.* Barbara Campbell, trans. Maryknoll, N.Y.: Orbis Books, 1982. Brazil.

Boff, Leonardo. "Ecclesiogenesis: Ecclesial Basic Communities Re-Invent the Church." *Midstream* 20:4 (October 1981). From Council on Christian Unity, Box 1986, Indianapolis, Ind. 46206.

Castillo, Metosalem Q. *The Church in Thy House.* Manila, Philippines: Alliance Publishers, 1982. On house churches in the Bible and in the Philippines.

"Church Basic Communities in Latin America." *WCC Exchange,* no. 2 (May 1979). World Council of Churches, 150 route de Ferney, 1211 Geneva 20, Switzerland. 47 pp.

Fraser, Ian M. *The Fire Runs.* London: SCM Press, Ltd., 1975. Africa, Asia, and Latin America.

Schillebeeckx, Edward. "The Christian Community and Its Office-Bearers." *Concilium.* New York: The Seabury Press, May 1980.

Torres, Sergio and Eagleson, John, eds. *The Challenge of Basic Christian Communities.* John Drury, trans. Maryknoll, N.Y.: Orbis Books, 1981. Papers from the International Ecumenical Congress of Theology, February 20 to March 2, 1980, Sao Paulo, Brazil.

Worship

Emswiler, Sharon Neufer, and Emswiler, Thomas Neufer. *Wholeness in Worship.* New York: Harper & Row, 1980.

Willimon, William H., and Wilson, Robert L. *Preaching and Worship in the Small Church.* Creative Leadership Series. Lyle Schaller, ed. Nashville: Abingdon, 1980.

Music

Glory & Praise: Songs for Christian Assembly. 3 vols. Phoenix, Arizona: North American Liturgy Resources, 1977, 1980, 1983.

Hymnal for Young Christians. 3 vols. Los Angeles: FEL Publications, 1966ff.
Sing and Rejoice! Orlando Schmidt, ed. Scottdale, Pa.: Herald Press, 1979.
Songs of Praise. 4 vols. Ann Arbor, Michigan: Servant Music, 1975ff.

Teaching and Learning with Children and Adults

Becker, Palmer and Ardys. *Creative Family Worship.* Worship Series, no. 15. Newton, Kansas: Faith and Life Press, and Scottdale, Pa.: Mennonite Publishing House, 1984.

Haessly, Jacqueline. *Peacemaking: Family Activities for Justice and Peace.* New York: Paulist Press, 1980.

Harder, Bertha Fast. *Celebrate! Ideas for Intergenerational Celebration of Advent/Christmas and Lent/Easter.* Newton, Kans.: Faith and Life Press, 1980.

Harder, Bertha, and Kropf, Marlene. *Intergenerational Learning in the Church.* Newton, Kans.: Faith and Life Press, 1982.

Lehn, Cornelia. *Involving Children and Youth in Congregational Worship.* Worship Series, no. 11. Newton, Kans.: Faith and Life Press, and Scottdale, Pennsylvania: Mennonite Publishing House, 1982.

McGinnis, Kathleen and James. *Parenting for Peace and Justice.* Maryknoll, N.Y.: Orbis Books, 1981.

_____. *Christian Parenting for Peace and Justice; Program Guide.* Nashville: Discipleship Resources, n.d.

Nutting, R. Ted. *Family Cluster Programs: Resources for Intergenerational Bible Study.* Valley Forge, Pa.: Judson Press, 1977.

Sawin, Margaret M. *Family Enrichment with Family Clusters.* Valley Forge, Pa.: Judson Press, 1979.

Sawin, Margaret M. *Family Enrichment with Family Clusters.* Valley Forge, Pa.: Judson Press, 1979.

Shelly, Maynard. *Discovery Bible Survey Course.* 4 vols. Newton, Kans.: Faith and Life Press, 1984, 1985.

Try This: Family Adventures Toward Shalom. Ecumenical Task Force on Christian Education for World Peace. Nashville: Discipleship Resources, 1979.

Welty, Lavon, ed. *Life Planning Manual.* Contains a coordinator's guide, advocates' guide, and packets for grades nine through twelve.) Order direct from Mennonite Board of Congregational Ministaries, Box 1245, Elkhart, Ind. 46515.

Wink, Walter. *Transforming Bible Study: A Leader's Guide.* Nashville: Abingdon, 1980.

Sharing

Griffin, Em. *Getting Together: A Guide for Groups.* Downers Grove, Ill.: InterVarsity Press, 1982.

Leslie, Robert C. *Sharing Groups in the Church.* Nashville: Abingdon, 1971.

Discipling

Devers, Dorothy. *Faithful Friendship.* By the author, 1979. Reprinted 1980 by Forward Movement Publications, 412 Sycamore Street, Cincinnati, Ohio 45202.

Foster, Richard J. *Celebration of Discipline.* San Francisco: Harper & Row, 1978.

Jeschke, Marlin. *Discipling the Brother: Congregational Discipline According to the Gospel.* Scottdale, Pa.: Herald Press, 1979.

Martin, John R. *Ventures in Discipleship: A Handbook for Groups or Individuals.* Scottdale, Pa.: Herald Press, 1984.

O'Connor, Elizabeth. *Journey Inward, Journey Outward.* New York: Harper & Row, 1968.

——————. *Search for Silence.* Waco: Word Books, 1972.

Spiker, Louise. *No Instant Grapes in God's Vineyard.* Valley Forge: Judson Press, 1982.

Yoder, John H. "Binding and Loosing." *Concern,* no. 14 (February 1967), pp. 2-32.

Decisions

Bartel, Barry C. *Communication Skills and Conflict Resolution.* Newton, Kans.: Faith and Life Press, 1983. Student guide and leader's guide.

Likert, Rensis, and Likert, Jane Gibson. *New Ways of Managing Conflict.* New York: McGraw-Hill, 1976.

Gifts

Becker, Palmer. *You and Your Options.* Rev. ed. Newton, Kans.: Faith and Life Press, 1983. A workbook.

Bittlinger, Arnold. *Gifts and Ministries.* Grand Rapids, Mich.: William B. Eerdmans Publishing Company, 1973. A study of the New Testament passages on gifts.

Contributing: Helping Others Fulfill Their Potential. San Bernardino, Calif.: Churches Alive! 1979. A study guide for groups. Leader's guide available.

O'Connor, Elizabeth. *Eighth Day of Creation: Gifts and Creativity.* Waco, Tex.: Word Books, 1971.

Woodrow, Peter. *Clearness: Processes for Supporting Individuals and Groups in Decision Making.* Philadelphia: Movement for a New Society. n.d.

Yoder, John H. "The Fullness of Christ: Perspectives on Ministries in Renewal." *Concern,* no. 17 (February 1969), pp. 33-93.

Mission

Mellis, Charles J. *Committed Communities: Fresh Streams for World Mission.* South Pasadena, Calif.: William Carey Library, 1976.

O'Connor, Elizabeth. *The New Community.* New York: Harper & Row, 1976.

Webber, George W. *The Congregation in Mission: Emerging Structures for the Church in an Urban World.* Nashville: Abingdon Press, 1964.

____________. *Today's Church: A Community of Exiles and Pilgrims.* Nashville: Abingdon, 1979.

Growing

Olsen, Charles M. *The Base Church: Creating Community Through Multiple Forms.* Atlanta: Forum House Publishers, 1973.

Rohr, Richard. "All of Life Together Is a Stage." *Sojourners* 10:2 (February 1981), pp. 17-19.

Periodicals for House Churches

Coming Together: A Journal About Christian Community. Published six times a year at 414 West Wolf, Elkhart, Ind., by the Shalom Covenant Communities. Subscription by donation ($10 suggested).

Gathering. Published six times a year by Leaven Press, Box 40292, Kansas City, Mo. 64141. Subscription: $10 a year.

Sojourners. Published monthly except August-September, at 1321 Otis Street NE, Box 29272, Washington, D.C. 20017. Subscription: $15 a year.

The House Church. Published four times a year at Newton, Kansas. Subscription: $3.50 per year. Subscription office: Box 964, Hesston, Kans. 67062.

The Other Side. Published every five weeks (except January and July) by Jubilee, Inc., 300 W. Apsley St., Philadelphia, Pa. 19144. Subscription: $19.75 per year.

The Small Group Letter. Published ten times a year by The Navigators. Subscription services at Box 1164, Dover, N.J. 07801; $17 a year.

The Author

Lois Barrett writes about house churches out of her experience in house churches, small groups within the church, and intentional community over the past fifteen years. She is currently mentor (teaching minister) of Mennonite Church of the Servant, a congregation of five house churches in Wichita, Kansas.

Lois's articles on house churches and other aspects of church life have appeared in numerous Christian periodicals, as well as in *The House Church* newsletter, of which she has been editor. She is the author of *The Vision and the Reality: The Story of Home Missions in the General Conference Mennonite Church*, published by Faith and Life Press in 1983. She was associate editor of *The Mennonite* from 1971 to 1977 and had previous experience writing for daily newspapers.

Born in Enid, Oklahoma, she lived in Kansas and Texas before graduating from the University of Oklahoma. She has since received a master of divinity degree from Mennonite Biblical Seminary, Elkhart, Indiana.

Lois currently serves on the executive council of the Institute of Mennonite Studies, Elkhart, Indiana, and the steering committee of Churches United for Peacemaking, Wichita, Kansas. She lives in Wichita with her husband, Thomas B. Mierau, and their children, Barbara, Susanna, and John.